For Freedom & Honour

G. L. Esson

Dedication

**This book is dedicated to the men and boys of
South Ronaldsay who went away to war and
did not return**

ISBN 0 9531563 5 4

Copyright George L. Esson 2001

Map of Western Front
Copyright Arthur Banks 1973

Pictures of the HMS Opal and Narborough
Courtesy of the Imperial War Museum, London

Published by Information PLUS,
Finstown, Orkney, KW17 2LH

Printed by The Orcadian,
Hell's Half Acre, Kirkwall.

They shall grow not old, as we that are left grow old

Age shall not weary them, nor the years condemn

At the going down of the sun, and in the morning

We will remember them.

Contents

Acknowledgements

I am grateful to a number of people for their help in the research and production of this record.

In particular I must acknowledge the help given by the following people:

Brian Budge, Richard Shearer, Allan Taylor and *Nicol Manson* of Kirkwall. *Alex T. Annal, Captain W. S. Banks, Roy Allan, Walter Forrest, Ann Stevenson* and the *local families* concerned.

David Bews and *Captain Sutherland Manson* of Thurso. *Jack Alexander* of Edinburgh and also the staff of the *Kirkwall Library.*

For permission to reproduce the map of the Western Front, I am grateful to *Arthur Banks* and *Pen and Sword Books Ltd.* Also *The Imperial War Museum* for the use of pictures of the HMS Opal and Narborough.

Last but not least, I must thank *my daughter Helen.* Without her help this record would never have been written.

George Esson

SOUTH RONALDSAY

TO COMMEMORATE AND HONOUR THE MEN OF SOUTH RONALDSHAY WHO FELL IN THE GREAT WAR.

L-CPL	WILLIAM CUMMING	Seaforth Highlanders
PTE	WILLIAM DASS	Seaforth Highlanders
PTE	MAGNUS DEARNESS	Seaforth Highlanders
PTE	WILLIAM ESSON	Seaforth Highlanders
PTE	ROBERT GUNN	Seaforth Highlanders
PTE	ROBERT HENDERSON	Seaforth Highlanders
PTE	WILLIAM MACDONALD	Seaforth Highlanders
PTE	JOHN H. N. ANNAL	Gordon Highlanders
L-CPL	JOHN MACKENZIE	Gordon Highlanders
PTE	JOHN D. CORMACK	Scots Guards
CPL	WILLIAM PETRIE	Scots Guards
SGT	JOSEPH THOMSON	Scots Guards
CSM	MAGNUS NORQUAY	Highland Light Infantry
PTE	WILLIAM DUNCAN	Northumberland Fusiliers
L-CPL	ARCHIBALD SINCLAIR	Machine Gun Corps
PTE	RICHARD SPENCE	Machine Gun Corps
GNR	WILLIAM BRUCE	Royal Garrison Artillery
GNR	JAMES SUTHERLAND	Royal Garrison Artillery
CPL	JAMES DUNNETT	Royal Engineers
PTE	DONALD NORQUAY	NZ Expeditionary Force
PTE	JOHN R. MARWICK	NZ Expeditionary Force
PTE	ROBERT SUTHERLAND	Canadian Expeditionary Force
PTE	GILBERT O. THOMSON	Canadian Expeditionary Force
PTE	WILLIAM R. CROMARTY	USA Expeditionary Force
DKH	JOHN BROWN	RN Reserve (Trawlers)
DKH	JOHN G.H. THOMSON	RN Mercantile Marine Reserve
ENG	JOHN SIMPSON	HM Transport Service

ALSO DIED ON ACTIVE SERVICE

1939 - 1945

PRIVATE	JOHN S. DOULL	Gordon Highlanders
SEAMAN	JOHN M. GUNN	RN Volunteer Reserve
SEAMAN	MAGNUS HENDERSON	Merchant Navy
SERGEANT	ROBERT MATHIESON	Royal Air Force
LEADING SEAMAN	JAMES RUSSELL	Royal Navy
2ND OFFICER	WILLIAM S. ROSIE	Merchant Navy
SEAMAN	WALTER SINCLAIR	Merchant Navy
DRIVER	DAVID SINCLAIR	Tank Corps
CAPTAIN	ANDREW THOMSON	Merchant Navy
SEAMAN	WILLIAM ROSIE	Merchant Navy

(This is the order in which their stories appear throughout the text.)

Introduction

This book is not intended to be anything more than an attempt to record the lives and deeds of the local servicemen who lost their lives in the two world wars.

This would certainly have been easier fifteen or twenty years ago when there were still survivors of the 1914-18 War alive who knew the men and perhaps had served and fought with them.

On the other hand, in recent years many books have been published on the different battles and campaigns. The internet has also been a good source of information.

The local families have been helpful with the loan of photographs and letters and have been keen to see a record made of the lives of the men.

In some instances it was just by good fortune that I was able to obtain photographs for now the people who had them are gone and the material is no longer available.

Having made every effort to verify the dates and details contained in this record there may be inaccuracies in the information for which I apologise.

The Great War

On the 11th of November 1918 the guns on the Western Front fell silent. Armistice had been signed at Compiègne in France and the Great War came at last to an end.

There had been a very high price to pay for this victory. Some idea of this can be gleaned from the casualty figures for the Battle of the Somme which started on 1st July 1916. British casualties in the battle numbered 400,000 and during the first day, the British Army on the Somme suffered 57,450 casualties of whom 20,000 were dead. The trench warfare of course went on continually.

The British Army was also engaged on other fronts, such as the Dardanelles and Mesopotamia. Reinforcements arrived from the Dominions with large numbers from Australia, Canada, New Zealand and South Africa.

The Royal Navy was, of course, fully committed in keeping the sea lanes open and permitting the passage of vital food and war supplies to enter the country. On the 30th May 1916 the British Grand Fleet under Admiral Lord Jellicoe left Scapa Flow to intercept the German High Sea Fleet and on the 31st May the first shots of the epic Battle of Jutland were fired. When the battle ended both sides claimed victory. The British Fleet lost more ships than the enemy and therefore could be said to have lost the battle. The German Fleet returned to its base and remained there for most of the war. The German High Sea Fleet was no longer a threat and the British Grand Fleet was left in control of the seas.

It has been said that by the time the conflict ended, there was hardly a home in the country that had not in some way been touched by dreadful effects of the war. The very best of British manhood had gone to the trenches of France and Flanders and to sea. South Ronaldsay was of course no different from the rest of the country.

It will be seen that local men fell in many of the major battles and campaigns of the war, Loos, Arras, Ypres, Festubert, Messine and the Somme. All claimed their lives, as well as the campaigns in Mesopotamia, Palestine and Italy.

The first local casualty occurred on the 1st of December 1914 and was the only one for that year. In 1915 three men died for King and Country. In 1916, the total for the year came to six with one man being killed on each of the three consecutive months of March, April and May.

1917, again, had a total of three casualties but 1918, the last year of the war, must have been the most traumatic with a total of fourteen local men falling to the gas, bullets and shells of the enemy. There is no doubt that the month of March 1918 must have been a most distressing period when the news came that four young men had been killed. The first was on the 4th when Engineer John Simpson lost his life at sea. On the 21st Private W. Duncan, 22nd Private J. Annal and on the 28th Private J. Cormack all fell during the big offensive by the enemy which started on the 21st March.

October saw another three men paying the price of freedom. Lance Corporal A. Sinclair and Private R. Spence, both machine gunners, were killed on the Western Front and Gunner W. Bruce died in the Middle East.

After the war ended, demobilisation began and the servicemen began to return home and settle back into civilian life.

The unveiling of the 1939-45 plaque – 5th September, 1948.

The South Ronaldsay War Memorial

In 1921 a branch of the British Legion was formed on the Island, but before this, some of the men had joined the Comrades of the Great War.

No doubt it was at meetings of these Organisations that thoughts turned to comrades who had made the supreme sacrifice and would not return home. In every island plans were being made for the erection of war memorials with the names of the fallen inscribed in stone so that they would never be forgotten. In South Ronaldsay, we were fortunate in obtaining the services of the sculptor, Mr. Alex Carrick ARSA, of Edinburgh. His mother was Elizabeth Harold Leith of the well known local family John Leith and Son, Drapers and Tailors.

Mr. Carrick was born in Musselburgh in 1882 and he served an apprenticeship with Birnie Rhind, an Edinburgh sculptor. He did replacement stone work for St Magnus Cathedral after setting up in his own business in Edinburgh. He was a regular exhibitor at the Royal Scottish Academy and was elected an Associate in 1919. He served in France with the Royal Artillery during the war so he would have been delighted when he was asked to create the bronze reliefs to the Royal Artillery and Royal Engineers for the Scottish National War Memorial at Edinburgh Castle. He was also responsible for the Wallace statue at the gateway to the castle. He created the War Memorials at Ayr, Berwick-on-Tweed, Dornoch, Forres, Fraserburgh,

Killin and our now familiar statue of a Seaforth Highlander in marching order. The statue itself with the tablet below are of Corstorphine stone. No doubt he would have taken great pride in carving the statue for the War Memorial on the island of his mother's birth.

The stonework (platform, pillars and base) was built of red and white boulders and was completed by John Norquay, Mason, of Herston.

The statue was based on a photograph of Private Robert McLaughlin of the Black Watch who was killed on the Somme in 1915.

The South Ronaldsay War Memorial Committee was formed with Mr. Barclay as Honorary Secretary. It appears to have carried out its duties very well. On the 2nd November 1921 it handed over the balance of £48-16-0 to the South Ronaldsay Parish Council to be used for the upkeep of the Memorial in the future.

The South Ronaldsay War Memorial as it stands now is arguably one of the finest in Orkney and is a fitting memorial to the 37 brave men whose names appear on it. Of the 37 names listed, 27 refer to the First World War and 10 to the Second World War. It will be noted that the list for the Second World War contains the names of members of the Merchant Navy, whereas they do not appear on the First World War list. The exact number of men who lost their lives while serving with the Merchant Navy during the war cannot be determined now but three have been identified.

Seaman William Budge of No 1 Cleat lost his life on the 9th February 1918 when his ship, the SS Express (W Cooper & Co of Kirkwall) was in collision with the British destroyer HMS Grenville near the Pentland Skerries. The entire crew of the Express was lost. She had been on passage from Leith to Kirkwall with a general cargo. William Budge was 19 years of age.

Seaman Magnus S Norquay of Stews, East Side lost his life by accident on 26th March 1915 when his ship, the SS Tynemouth, was docked at Cardiff. He was 20 years of age.

Thirty-one year old Alexander H Sinclair of Kirkhouse, East Side lost his life when sailing as Master of the 73 ton two masted topsail schooner Janet. She left the Firth of Forth on 6th November 1918, bound for Orkney, just five days before the end of hostilities and was never heard of again.

The fate of the Janet was never established. She may have struck a mine or she may have become the prey of an enemy ship or submarine. It is also possible that the weather may have been responsible. The Janet was armed with one gun and carried one Royal Navy gunner. The crew members were Alex H Sinclair,

Master, the mate was a Guthrie man from Burray and two seamen, J Burghes from Stronsay and Henry Stevenson from Berriedale, Westray.

She was owned by Captain P S Cooper of Kirkwall at the time of her loss.

In addition to the 27 names which appear on the memorial, there is one that does not. He was a 17 year old boy from St Margaret's Hope who served with the Mercantile Marine Reserve on board HMS Imperieuse and he lost his life on the 7th March 1918. He was Deckhand Alexander Brown, and his parents were Alexander and Elizabeth Brown of Back Road, St Margaret's Hope. He was buried in the North Churchyard in a grave marked with a Commonwealth War Graves Commission headstone.

After the war had ended, the next-of-kin were sent the medals which the soldier would have been entitled to had he survived. They were the British War Medal and the Victory Medal. In November 1918 the King awarded a decoration, a Star in Bronze, to men who had served in Belgium and France under Field Marshal Sir John French between 5th August and 22nd November 1914. These were the men who served in what the Kaiser called General French's Contemptible Little Army, and who thereafter were referred to with pride as "The Old Contemptibles". In December 1918 the King awarded a similar decoration, the 1914-1915 Star, to men from any branch of the armed forces who had served King and Country between the 5th August 1914 and the 31st December 1915, but men who were eligible for the 1914 Star would not receive the second award. They were also sent a bronze plaque, about $4^3/4''$ in diameter. This plaque bore the figure of Britannia and a lion with the man's name and the words "He died for Freedom and Honour". These plaques are sometimes referred to as "The Death Penny".

The ceremony of Unveiling and Dedication of the South Ronaldsay War Memorial took place on Sunday 21st August 1921. In the morning, ex-servicemen assembled at the East End Hall and, commanded by Major Buchanan, marched to St Margaret's Church. The parade was headed by the Kirkwall City Pipe Band. After the church service, which was attended by 600 people, the parade marched to the War Memorial when the Unveiling and Dedication took place. The Unveiling was carried out by Miss Jessie Sutherland on behalf of her mother who had lost two sons in the war and had one severely wounded.

The Dedication Address was delivered by the Rev JSW Irvine, followed by "The Flowers of the Forest" , played by the Pipe Band. The "Last Post" was sounded by trumpeter D Wooldrage. The officiating clergy at the ceremony were Rev JSW Irvine, Rev A Goodfellow, Rev J Forbes MA and Rev W Baldwin.

The items which follow on the individual servicemen are listed in the same order in which they appear on the War Memorial.

The Seaforth Highlanders

The regiment known as the Seaforth Highlanders was raised in 1778 by Kenneth MacKenzie, Earl of Seaforth, who took his title from Loch Seaforth on the island of Lewis. The new regiment was known as the 78th Highlanders, later renumbered to 72nd. Its first tour of duty was to the Channel Islands where it twice opposed French attempts to capture the islands. Its next posting was to India where it remained for years in the service of the East India Company.

Over the years the regiment served in many parts of the Empire including the North West Frontier of India. It also fought in the Crimean War and the Boer War.

On the outbreak of the Great War on 4th August 1914, the 1st Battalion Seaforth Highlanders was stationed at Agra in India and was quickly moved to France, arriving there in October 1914 as part of the Dehra Dun Brigade, 7th Meerut Division, Indian Expeditionary Force. The Battalion's first actions on the Western Front were at Richebourg St Vaast, Neuve Chapelle and Festubert during the winter of 1914-15. On the 9th May 1915 it fought at Aubers Ridge and suffered over 500 casualties in the unsuccessful attack. Because of the heavy losses, the Battalion was held in reserve for some time.

In November 1915 the 1st Seaforths, with the 7th Meerut Division, left the Western Front and sailed to Basra in

Mesopotamia, arriving there on Christmas Day. Its first action involved a voyage up the River Tigris and then a march to Kut-el-Amara where Indian Army troops were besieged by the Turks. The Battalion suffered very heavy casualties at Sheikh Saad, Umm-el-Hannah and Wadi. The attacks were made across open country, completely at the mercy of the Turkish rifles and machine guns. The second Battalion Black Watch suffered similar losses and on the 4th February 1916 the two Battalions were amalgamated and were known as the Highland Battalion. This arrangement continued until 12th July when reinforcements to both battalions arrived from the UK. Several desperate attempts were made to relieve the besieged garrison at Kut but, under General Townsend, it surrendered to the Turks on 29th April. Both sides were exhausted and the hot summer months were spent resting and rebuilding the shattered forces.

By March 1917, the 1st Seaforths had advanced and after 14 days hard marching was part of the force which captured Baghdad on 11th March. The advance continued beyond the city until the railway was in British hands.

Towards the end of 1917 the Battalion moved back to Basra and on 1st January it embarked for Egypt where it spent some time resting and refitting to be ready for its next campaign. It then joined General Allenby's force in Palestine and on 26th September took part in its last action of the war, the capture of Beit Lid. Private Magnus Dearness was killed in action and Private Thomas Kent of Westray and Private Thomas Loutit of Holm lost their lives as a result of wounds received in the Beit Lid action.

During the inter-war years, the 1st Seaforths served in Ireland, Palestine, Egypt and Hong Kong. The 2nd Battalion served in India with some time spent on the North West Frontier, and later served in Palestine before returning to the United Kingdom.

At the outbreak of the 2nd World War on 3rd September 1939, the 1st Seaforth Battalion was in Shanghai where it remained until August 1940 when it moved to Singapore and then to Penang. From 1942 - 1944 the Battalion fought in Assam and Burma. After $2^{1}/_{2}$ years of active service the Battalion returned to India.

All Battalions of the Seaforth Highlanders fought throughout the Second World War as they did throughout the First War, with great valour and distinction.

Other Battalions fought through the North African Campaign in battles from El Alamein to Tripoli, to the Wadi Akarit and on to Sicily. Some Battalions then returned to Britain to train for the Normandy landings and the fierce fighting which followed, leading ultimately to the Rhine Crossings and the final advance into the heart of Germany.

Having fought through the 2 World Wars, the Seaforth Highlanders became a victim of a round of government spending cuts. On 7th February 1961, at Redford Barracks, Edinburgh, the Regiment was amalgamated with the Queens Own Cameron Highlanders and the new Regiment was known as the Queens Own Highlanders. Again on 17th September 1994, the Queens Own Highlanders and the Gordon Highlanders were amalgamated at Dreghorn Barracks, Edinburgh. The new Regiment is known as The Highlanders.

The Seaforth Highlanders were for many years regarded as being "Orkney's Regiment". The Regiment recruited locally with vigour and many young Orcadians joined the Regiment and, as can be seen from a study of any war memorial, many did not return.

Chronological list of casualties WW1

1914 1 December L/Cpl John Mackenzie 1st Gordon Highlanders

1915 22 April Pte Gilbert Thomson 2nd Canadians
 16 May CSM Magnus Norquay 9th Highland Light Infantry
 7 October L/Cpl William Cumming 8th Seaforth Highlanders

1916 30 March Cpl William Petrie 1st Scots Guards
 19 April Sgt Joseph Thomson 2nd Scots Guards
 3 May Pte Robert Gunn 8th Seaforth Highlanders
 1 August Pte William Esson 1st Seaforth Highlanders
 15 August Deckhand John G H Thomson RNMMR
 30 September Pte Robert Sutherland 8th Canadians

1917 22 February Pte William Dass 1st Seaforth Highlanders
 25 May Pte William MacDonald 2nd Seaforth Highlanders
 21 June Pte Donald Norquay 2nd NZ Rifles

1918 4 March Engineer John Simpson HM Transport Service
 21 March Pte William Duncan 25th Northumberland Fusiliers
 22 March Pte John Annal 6th Gordon Highlanders
 28 March Pte John Cormack 2nd Scots Guards
 7 July Pte Robert Henderson 4th Seaforth Highlanders
 13 August Deckhand John Brown RNR (T)
 11 September Pte William Cromarty 77th "Statue of Liberty" Div.
   US Exp Force
 20 September Pte Magnus Dearness 1st Seaforth Highlanders
 1 October L/Cpl Archibald Sinclair 219th Coy, Machine Gun Corps
 12 October Pte Richard Spence Machine Gun Corps
   Cavalry Squadron
 29 October Gunner William Bruce Royal Garrison Artillery
 5 November Pte John Marwick 2nd New Zealanders
 25 November Cpl James Dunnett Royal Engineers
 31 December Gunner James Sutherland Royal Garrison Artillery

Lance Corporal William Cumming

S6342 Lance Corporal William Cumming served with the 8th Battalion Seaforth Highlanders, 44th Brigade, 15th Scottish Division. The 44th Brigade was composed of 8th Seaforth, 9th Black Watch, 10th Gordons and 7th Cameron Highlanders. His home was at Bayview, Sandwick and his parents were James and Robina Cumming (née Rosie.)

Before enlisting in the army he worked on one of Robert Garden's floating shops. He was a volunteer soldier and he enlisted in Kirkwall.

The 15th Scottish was a newly formed Division and, with the exception of senior officers and some regular NCO's, they were volunteers to a man. They had answered Lord Kitchener's call to arms. They had responded to his famous poster with the pointing finger and the caption *"Your King and Country Needs You."* They were part of Kitchener's second hundred thousand, his 2nd Army, K2. Although the 15th Scottish was a new and inexperienced division, they were very well trained and the men were young and fit.

The 44th Brigade left for France on 7th July 1915 and crossed from Folkestone to Boulogne, and over a period of some days made their way to the front line where they soon gained experience of trench warfare and suffered their first casualties.

Their first major action was at the Battle of Loos on Saturday 25th September 1915. The battle had been preceded by an artillery barrage which continued for four days and nights. At 0550hrs chlorine gas was released, and at 0630hrs the main assault commenced and the Seaforth Highlanders went "over the top." This was the first time that gas was used by the British Army.

On the morning of the 25th it was thought that weather conditions were favourable but unfortunately that was not what happened. In parts of the front line the gas moved slowly over to the enemy positions, causing panic in the German trenches. In other parts it hung around in "no man's land" and some of it blew back into the British trenches.

The 15th Scottish had to advance on a 1500 yard front and the 8th Seaforths, from their starting positions between Grenay and Vermelles, advanced over flat open ground without any cover, completely at the mercy of the enemy machine guns. They had been given as their objectives the capture of the enemy first and second line trenches, the capture of Loos village, an advance on to Hill 70 and to occupy Cite St Auguste.

Many brave Highlanders fell in front of the enemy trenches. They were met by a formidable barrier of barbed wire which had not been destroyed by the artillery. The wire was 4 feet high and from 10 to 20 yards deep.

It could be said that the Battle of Loos was a battle of lost opportunities. The advances and objectives won by the infantry at great cost could not be properly exploited. The Generals had planned the battle without ensuring that the reserves were close enough to the front line to secure the ground won.

By 0800hrs the enemy trenches had been taken and after house-to-house fighting, Loos village was in British hands along with a battery of German field guns. The advance up Hill 70 continued until it was captured by 0845hrs. The Highlanders stayed on Hill 70 until they were relieved at 0245hrs on the 27th.

Casualties suffered by the 8th Seaforths on the three days - 25th, 26th & 27th September - were 19 officers and 700 other ranks.

On the 27th September 1915, a message was received by the 15th Scottish Division.

"The Corps Commander is anxious that you should communicate to all ranks of the 15th Division his high appreciation of the admirable fighting spirit which they displayed in the attack and capture of Loos village and Hill 70. Sir Douglas Haig has also desired the Corps Commander to convey his congratulations to the Division. The Major General wishes to say that he is very proud of his command."
Signed J.T.Burnett-Stuart. Lt Col General Staff.

A brigadier at the end of his report on the battle wrote:

"This brief summary cannot be closed without some slight testimony to the extraordinary fighting spirit displayed by all ranks. Every officer and man was doing his utmost and nothing would have stopped them getting through. Nothing could have surpassed the dash and fury with which the brigade captured the German front trenches. It is a fact well worth recording when it is remembered that a year before the profession of arms was foreign to most of the men."

Lance Corporal Cumming died on 7th October 1915 from wounds received on Hill 70 and he is buried in Grave 7A, Row C, Plot 3, Etaples Military Cemetery, France.

Private William Dass

S13328 Private William Dass was one of three South Ronaldsay men who died while serving with the 1st Battalion Seaforth Highlanders, 19th Indian Brigade, 7th Meerut Division. The 19th Indian Brigade was comprised of the 1st Seaforths, 28th Punjabis, 92nd Punjabis and the 125th Napier's Rifles from its arrival in Mesopotamia in January 1916 until the end of the war. An Indian Brigade usually consisted of one British and three Indian Battalions with British Officers.

His home was at Brain, East Side, and his parents were William and Euphemia Dass (née Petrie). He worked at home and went inshore fishing. He was born on 13th September 1896. He was a volunteer soldier and enlisted in South Ronaldsay.

The 1st Battalion Seaforth Highlanders arrived in Mesopotamia (now called Iraq) in January 1916 after spending a year in France. Mesopotamia was vital to Britain, being the source of much of the oil needed for the war effort. The British Government had a controlling interest in the Anglo Persian Oil Company which produced it.

During the early part of 1916 the 1st Battalion Seaforths suffered heavy casualties during the attacks on the Turks at Sheikh Saad on 7th January, at Wadi on 13th January and again at Umm-el-Hannah on 21st and 22nd January.

On the 22nd February 1917 the 1st Battalion took part in an attack on the Turkish position at Sannaiyat, capturing three lines of enemy trenches. It was in this action that Private William Dass lost his life. He was one of two local soldiers who went to Mesopotamia with the 1st Seaforths and did not return. In the action at Sannaiyat they had been supported by 36 machine guns, 70 guns firing in enfilade, several Field Batteries and a large number of 2 inch and Stokes mortars. The final attack was, of course, up to the infantry and that must have been when Private Dass fell.

The following item appeared in "Our Roll of Honour" of the Orcadian at the time of his death.

The sad news of the death of Private William Dass, Seaforth Highlander, was received by his parents last week. The War Secretary says that he was killed in action on the 22nd February at the Persian Gulf. Private Dass had been in Mesopotamia for a few months only, and had been sending home very cheery letters and had enjoyed his New Year's Day with others. All the time his health was good and he loved the beautiful country. No further word has been received about his death but he died nobly on the battlefield and made the supreme sacrifice. It may be mentioned Private Dass was only 20 years and 5 months old, and at home was a well-behaved and much respected young man.

He is commemorated on the Seaforth panels (37 and 64) of the Basra memorial.

Private Magnus Dearness

204227 Private Magnus Dearness served with the 1st Battalion Seaforth Highlanders, 19th Indian Brigade, 7th Meerut Division. His home was at Quoyangry and his parents were Robert and Jemima Dearness (née. Norquay). Before enlisting in the army he worked on the farm and went inshore fishing. He was born on 10th May 1898.

In March 1917 the Battalion took part in the capture of Baghdad and then fought actions to secure the railway system. It then spent the hot part of the year near the village of Samarra. At the end of 1917 the 1st Battalion moved back to Basra and on the 1st January 1918 it embarked for Egypt. They then had a period of rest and refitting at Ismalia before joining General Allenby's force in Palestine. At 4.30am on 19th September 1918, the 19th and 21st Brigades assaulted the Turkish defences to the west of Tabsor. The attack was successful and their objectives were quickly secured. By the evening both El Medzel and Taiyibrth had been taken.

On the 20th September the Battalion took part in what was to be its last action of the war. This was the attack on, and capture of, Beit Lid, which was a small village about 8 miles WNW of Nablus. It was in this action that Private Dearness lost his life. The action was successful but it was not without difficulties. At one point the advance was halted until water was found. A well was located at Kufr Zibad and the exhausted men were able to rest and drink. By 11am on the 20th, the 19th Brigade had advanced to within 1000 yards of Beit Lid, where they came under attack by an enemy battery. At 2pm the 1st Seaforths launched their final attack but they were stopped 200 yards short of the village, having suffered 120 casualties. Support came at 5.30pm from a battery of the VIII Mountain Artillery Brigade and Beit Lid was taken by the 28th Punjabis who cleared the village with grenades.

By the time the action was complete, the 7th Division had marched and fought over 34 miles in 48 hours in difficult country. All objectives were taken and 2000 prisoners and 20 guns were captured. Private Magnus Dearness was buried in Grave B6, Plot S, Ramleh War Cemetery, Palestine.

Private William Esson

S12439 Private William Esson served in Mesopotamia with the 1st Battalion Seaforth Highlanders, 19th Dehra Dun Brigade, 7th Meerut Division. His home was at Brandyquoy, Garth and his parents were John and Barbara Esson (née Berston). Before enlisting in the army, he worked at home on the farm. He was born on 31st October 1895. He was a volunteer soldier and he enlisted in South Ronaldsay.

Private Esson died of wounds in Mesopotamia on 1st August 1916. At that time the 1st Battalion was held in Divisional Reserve after a spell in the trenches at Sannaiyat. The men had been fighting and living in very difficult conditions with temperatures as high as 122° F, and at times 116°F in the tents. Because of the heat, there was little movement by either side. The garrison of Kut had surrendered on 29th April and the relief force had suffered crippling casualties in failed attempts to reach there.

There was a large number of men reporting sick with heat stroke, dysentery and other tropical diseases. The conditions were not good; hospital and rest camps were poorly equipped, letters from home were irregular due to the actions of the enemy U boats and leave was just about non-existent.

The campaign in Mesopotamia cost the British Empire 14,814 men killed in action, 12,807 died from disease and 52,000 were wounded. A total of 13,494 men were reported missing or as prisoners of the Turkish Army.

Private William Esson was buried in Grave 16, Row H, Plot 22, Amara War Cemetery.

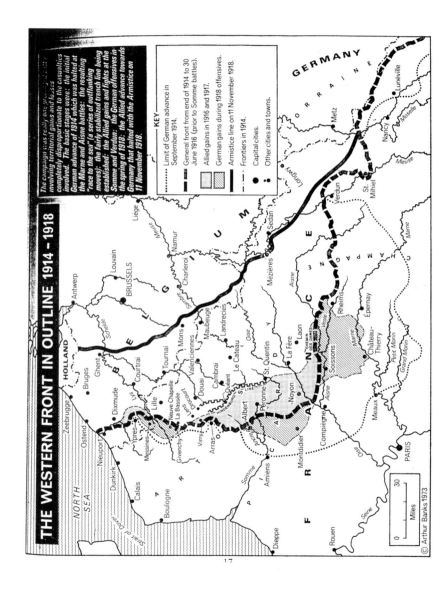

THE WESTERN FRONT IN OUTLINE 1914 – 1918

The campaign was really one prolonged battle involving territorial gains and losses completely disproportionate to the casualties involved. The basic stages were: the initial German advance of 1914 which was halted at the Marne and Aisne battles; the resulting "race to the sea" (a series of outflanking moves); the fairly stabilized trench line being established; the Allied gains and fights at the Somme and Verdun; the German offensives in the spring of 1918; the Allied advance towards Germany that halted with the Armistice on 11 November 1918.

— KEY —

············· Limit of German advance in September 1914.

▪▪▪▪ General front from end of 1914 to 30 June 1916 (prior to Somme battles).

▨ Allied gains in 1916 and 1917.

▨ German gains during 1918 offensives.

▪·▪·▪ Armistice line on 11 November 1918.

─·─ Frontiers in 1914.

● Capital cities.

· Other cities and towns.

© Arthur Banks 1973

0 30
Miles

Private Robert Gunn

S6531 Private Robert Gunn served with the 8th Battalion Seaforth Highlanders, 44th Brigade, 15th Division.

His home was at Herston and his parents were James and Christine Gunn (née Mowatt). He was born on 15th December 1892.

Before enlisting in the army he worked at Midtown, Herston. He was a volunteer soldier, having enlisted at St Margaret's Hope.

He was with the 8th Battalion at Hulluch Front, Loos and was the second local man to fall in the fighting in that area. He had been in France for a year and had been home on leave at the New Year. The 8th Seaforths were back on the Front Line on the 24th April 1916 when the 15th Division relieved the 12th Division in the Quarries and Hohenzollern sectors near Loos. They faced the 3rd Bavarian Division across No Man's Land. Between 5 and 6 on the morning of the 27th April the Germans released gas and exploded two mines under the British trenches and again on the 1st and 5th May another two mines were exploded. Private Robert Gunn lost his life on the 3rd May 1916.

Letters from Officers of his Regiment to his parents were published in the Orcadian at the time of his death. The Captain of Private Gunn's company wrote to the deceased's mother

"I was greatly grieved when your son was killed by a trench mortar on the night of 3rd May 1916. It was during a small bombing attack made by my company.

Your son was doing excellent work, he was indeed one of the best bombers in my company and was selected for a difficult piece of work. He was an excellent fighter and you have much to be proud of.

May you be consoled in your loss in that he died fighting, killed suddenly in the heat of battle. Please accept my sincere sympathy."

Second Lt. Duncan also wrote

"I must also write you and offer my deepest sympathy to you in your affliction. The sorrow of a mother's heart is too profound for an understanding, but it may lighten the weight of the sorrow to know that your son died fighting.

He was in the bombing section of my platoon and always showed a steadiness and devotion to duty which did not pass unappreciated. He lies near the spot where he fell fighting, his grave marked with a simple wooden cross which marks a warrior's grave. His comrades join with me in sending you our deepest sympathy. They miss him from the section as do I."

The Chaplain also wrote a very kind letter.

He is commemorated on Loos Memorial, Pas de Calais, France. Seaforth Highlanders are commemorated on panels 112 to 115 on this Memorial. Loos Memorial is part of Dud Corner Cemetery about 1 kilometre west of Loos-en-Gohelle village.

Private Robert Henderson

S17021 Private Robert Henderson served with the 4th Battalion Seaforth Highlanders, 154th Brigade, 51st Division. The 154th Brigade was composed of the 9th Royal Scots, 7th Argyll & Sutherland Highlanders, 4th Gordon and 4th Seaforth Highlanders. His home was at East Shaird, Sandwick and his parents were William and Jane Henderson (née Leith). He was born on 20th May 1898. He was a volunteer soldier, having enlisted in Kirkwall.

Private Henderson died in the Royal Victoria Hospital Southampton on 17th July 1918 from wounds received in France. He was the only local soldier from the First World War to be buried at home. His grave is in the North Churchyard and is marked with a Commonwealth War Graves Commission headstone. His funeral was well attended by Marines and civilians.

The 4th Seaforths arrived in France on 6th November 1914. Their first major action was on 10th March at Neuve Chapelle where they suffered 168 casualties. They saw action again at Aubers Ridge in May 1915; The Somme in 1916 and The Ancre also in 1916. This was the last phase of the Battle of the Somme and during this battle the 51st Division took part in the capture of Beaumont Hammel.

Private Henderson's wounds were reported in The Orcadian

of 22nd September 1917. The 4th Seaforths were out of the line from 8th to 29th August, so it is likely that he was wounded sometime on or after 29th August 1917, but he could have been the victim of a random shell at any time. Shelling by both sides went on continually and men who were at some distance from the front line could become victims. At this time the enemy had air superiority and frequent bombing raids were made on the British lines.

When the Battalion returned to the Front Line, they arrived at the start of the second phase of the Third Battle of Ypres. This was to become known as the Battle of Passchendale. The Front Line to the east of the Steenbeek was a mess of mud and water-filled shell holes, making it hard going for the infantry. On the 6th September the Battalion relieved the 6th Seaforths on the Front Line near Langemarck where the line was held by a series of isolated posts. On the 9th September they were relieved by the 7th Black Watch and went to Siege camp near Elverdinghe.

Wounded soldiers were carried from the battlefield by stretcher-bearers, and as soon as possible taken to a Regimental Aid Post. The stretcher-bearers were trained in first aid and could apply basic treatment. The casualties made their way from Main Dressing Stations to a Casualty Clearing Station which could be situated far behind the front line. Some of the CCSs specialised in certain injuries. One station would take gas cases and another chest wounds etc. They were then carried by ambulance or train to a Base Hospital. Many soldiers recovered from their wounds and returned to their Battalions.

The seriously wounded men were eventually repatriated to hospitals in Scotland or England, and this was what happened to Private Robert Henderson.

Private William MacDonald

S12488 Private William MacDonald served with the 2nd Battalion Seaforth Highlanders, 10th Brigade, 4th Division. The 10th Brigade consisted of the 2nd Seaforth Highlanders, 1st Royal Irish Fusiliers, 1st Royal Warwickshire Regiment and the Household Battalion.

His home was at Moss of Cletts, East Side, and his parents were Duncan and Isabella MacDonald (née Walls). He was born on 20th August 1881. He was a volunteer soldier and he enlisted at St Margaret's Hope.

The Second Seaforths, a Regular Army Battalion, was quickly mobilized on the outbreak of war, and landed at Boulogne on the 23rd August 1914. Their first major action was at Aisne 14th-30th September 1914, Meteren 13th October and Ploegsteert on the 7th November. They suffered very heavy casualties during the 2nd Battle of Ypres and again at Redan Ridge near Beaumont Hammel on the first day of the Battle of the Somme in 1916.

On the 10th April 1917, the 2nd Seaforths were in positions to the west of the village of Fampoux when they were ordered to attack the chemical works between Fampoux and Roeux. The target was well defended and the enemy soldiers were well aware of what was happening. A German aircraft had reported the situation to their comrades.

The Seaforths along with the 1st Royal Irish Fusiliers moved up a sunken road to Hyderabad Redoubt and then had to cross an area of open ground to reach the chemical works. They were immediately caught in heavy machine gun fire from the well-prepared defenders. Up to 30 machine guns were directed against the British soldiers and they had no chance of reaching their objective. The chemical works had not been subjected to an artillery barrage and the German soldiers were able to mow down the attacking British soldiers at will as they crossed the open ground. This was an action which should never have been contemplated and appears to have been very poorly planned.

Private William MacDonald died on the 25th May 1917 from wounds which he was likely to have received during the attack on the chemical works. The Highlanders suffered 375 casualties from the 432 who took part in the assault. After this action, the 2nd Seaforths were withdrawn from the front until reinforcements from the UK became available and were trained in trench warfare. On the 23rd April the chemical works fell into British hands when they were captured by the 4th Seaforth Highlanders of the 51st Highland Division.

A Second Lieutenant of the Seaforths wrote later:

"Right from the start it was a dreadful affair. A fine battalion totally destroyed. It was a total disgrace that the powers that be could order such an attack in full daylight against such

defences. We had no chance at all and I lost many good friends that day, including Duncan MacIntosh who of course won the Victoria Cross. I had only gone about 200 yards before I was shot through the chest. I am sorry, but I cannot talk about it any more."

The war diary of the 10th Brigade records: From Hyderabad Redoubt there is now a long row of dead Seaforth Highlanders visible where they were swept down by enemy machine gun fire.

Private William MacDonald was wounded and died on the 25th May 1917. He was buried in Plot 25, Row D, Grave 2, Etaples War Cemetery, which lies 27 kilometres south of Boulogne.

Private John H.N. Annal

S41097 Private John H N Annal served with the 6th Battalion Gordon Highlanders, 152nd Brigade, 51st Division. His home was at Lythes, East Side. He was married to Jane Tait and they had one daughter, Molly. His parents were James and Jane Annal (née Christie). John Annal was a volunteer soldier having enlisted at Fort George. Before joining the army he was a tailor.

Private John Annal was killed in action on 22nd March 1918 in the Boursies-Doignies area near St Quentin. On 21st March the Germans opened their spring offensive with Operation "Michael", intended to split the French and British armies before fresh American troops could be brought to the front.

The 6th Gordons were in the trenches near Boursies when at 4.45am on the morning of the 21st March, the Germans opened an intense bombardment of the Front, Support and Intermediate Lines with 5.9 inch, 8 inch and gas shells. At 11.30am, a large number of enemy were seen coming from Boursies and advancing down the Boursies-Doignies Road. All available rifles along with three Lewis guns opened fire and inflicted many casualties. The 51st (Highland) Division stood firm on the first day, but by nightfall on the 21st it had to withdraw before being encircled and cut off. On the 22nd March, orders were received to hold a line on the north side of the Bapaume-Cambrai Road.

There was fierce fighting in the area around St Quentin and of the 8 British Battalions that went into battle, only 50 men came back unscathed. The 6th Gordons suffered 240 casualties from 21st to 26th March in the Michael offensive.

Private John Annal is buried in Grave A, Row 2, Beaumetz-les-Cambrai Military Cemetery No 1, Pas-de-Calais, France.

Lance Corporal John MacKenzie

7754 Lance Corporal John MacKenzie served with the 1st Battalion Gordon Highlanders, 8th Brigade, 3rd Division

He was a volunteer soldier. His home was at Inkerman, Grimness and he was married to Catherine Cumming of Gimps. They had two of a family, John and Catherine. His parents were Archibald and Mary MacKenzie (née Annal) of Inkerman. Private MacKenzie was the first soldier belonging to South Ronaldsay to lose his life in the war.

The 1st Battalion Gordon Highlanders were stationed at Plymouth at the outbreak of war but they soon found themselves in the thick of it, having landed at Boulogne on the 14th August 1914. Their first action came on 23rd - 24th August at Mons then at Marne, La Bassee and 1st Ypres.

The 1st Gordons remained at the Ypres front during the winter of 1914-15. They were in the trenches near Hooge east of Ypres until the 20th November when they were relieved by a French unit. During their time at Hooge they had to contend with intermittent shelling and very bad weather conditions, heavy rain, snow and sleet resulting in several cases of frostbite. From the 21st -29th November they were in billets at Westoure and Locre. On the 30th November they were back in the trenches, this time near Kemmel on the right of the Kemmel-Wytschaete Road, where they took over from the 7th Fusiliers. The Battalion war Diary for the 1st December reads:- "Strength of Battalion 8 officers 459 other ranks. Trenches very wet. Casualties 1 man killed and 3 wounded." It appears from this that L-Cpl John MacKenzie must have been the Battalion's only fatality on that day.

He is commemorated on panel 38 of the Ypres (Menin Gate) Memorial, Belgium.

Private John D Cormack

16224 Private John D Cormack served with the 2nd Battalion Scots Guards, 3rd Guards Brigade, Guards Division.

His home was at Dundas House, South Parish and his parents were David M. and Margaret Cormack (née Taylor). Before joining the army he worked in the Co-operative shop in St Margaret's Hope. He was born on 9th February 1898.

He enlisted at Hoxa Head on 3rd June 1916 before Lt George Barclay and was mobilised on 28th November 1916. He was posted to Caterham for training where he qualified as a sniper. He landed at Le Havre in France on 14th August 1917, joining his Battalion in the field on 21st September.

Private Cormack was gassed when the 2nd Scots Guards were on the front line during the Battle of Cambrai in November 1917. He recovered from the effects of the gas and rejoined his Battalion near the French town of Elverdinge. They had a bad time in the trenches, at times they were up to the waist in mud and were shelled, machine-gunned and bombed. They also had to suffer gas attacks. It certainly was a baptism of fire for a young South Ronaldsay boy.

The German "Michael" offensive started on 21st March 1918 and the 2nd Battalion was in the front line on the 23rd March. Various Battalions and even whole Divisions were in retreat and the 2nd Battalion withdrew to the "Army Line." On the 26th they had posts pushed out as far as Boyelles and Boiry Becquerelles but were forced to retire fighting before the strong German advances. On the 27th they suffered badly from the enemy artillery.

Sadly he lost his life on 28th March 1918 when the 2nd Battalion Scots Guards found themselves back in the front line. The British Artillery delivered a heavy bombardment to the German positions but when it ended the Germans replied, causing severe losses to the 2nd Battalion's flanks.

The following item appeared in the South Ronaldsay District News of The Orcadian at the time of his death.

On the 28th March, Private John D Cormack of the Scots Guards fell on the Western Front at the age of 20. He is one of ourselves, and the first soldier of the South Parish to make the great sacrifice. After a severe training in England he was drafted to France and was gassed at Cambrai. He wrote home then saying it was surely by the grace of God that he came through that terrible struggle. Now in another great struggle he has perished. He fought for us, he suffered for us, he died for us, for his King and Country. Now we hold his name in everlasting remembrance. His mother and family, while they mourn the loss of such a son and brother, yet have cause to be proud of what he has done.

He is commemorated in Bay 1 of the Arras Memorial, France.

Private John D Cormack

Corporal William Petrie

11856 Corporal William Petrie served with the 1st Battalion Scots Guards, 2nd Guards Brigade, Guards Division

His home was at Lynegar, Hoxa and his parents were Alexander and Catherine Petrie (née Rosie).

Before joining the army he was a county labourer in West Lothian. He was a volunteer soldier joining on 31st October 1914 in Edinburgh. He commenced his training at Caterham on 3rd November 1914.

He arrived in France on 4th May 1915 and was listed 'missing' and then 'killed in action' on 30th March 1916.

At the time of his death, the 1st Battalion had moved to Ypres where it relieved the 2nd Battalion. They were in trenches with the 1st Coldstream Guards on their right and the 1st Guards Brigade on their left. The 30th March was a bad day in the trenches for the 1st Scots Guards. A German bombardment was concentrated on their area from 1.30pm to 7pm. Casualties for the day in the Battalion were 24 killed, 47 wounded, 8 missing and 20 men were admitted to field ambulance suffering from shock. All of these casualties were caused by artillery, as there was no action by infantry on that day. No doubt it was during this bombardment that Cpl. Petrie fell.

His parents received the following letter from the Sergeant Major of his Company in France. It was published in the Orcadian (dated 20th May 1916) at the time of his death.

"France 13.4.1916

Dear Mr & Mrs Petrie

I am writing to offer you on behalf of myself and the whole company our sincerest and deepest sympathy in the death of your son, Corporal Petrie. It may be of some little condolence to you all perhaps to know the circumstances of his death. He was, as you perhaps know, the N.C.O. in charge of our Lewis Gun. On the day he met his death we had suffered a very heavy bombardment, and on being relieved in the evening the Germans let us have it again. Your son was taking his gun out and was I know persuaded by several to leave it and get away himself, but his sense of duty would not allow him to abandon his gun and he was eventually killed by shell fire with his gun by his side. He died a hero's death in every sense of the word. He was greatly respected by the whole company and personally I had the highest opinion of him in every way.

He always did his duty thoroughly in every respect and nothing was too much trouble for him to undertake.

Under the most adverse weather conditions in the trenches he always had a smile and a cheery word and as he lived amongst

us all, so he died, doing his duty thoroughly till the very end."
He now lies in Grave 11, Row C, Potijze Burial Ground,
Belgium which lies North East of the town of Ypres.

Lance Sergeant Joseph Thomson

6747 Lance Sergeant Joseph Thomson served with the 2nd Battalion Scots Guards, 3rd Guards Brigade, Guards Division.

His parents were Robert and Isabella Thomson and their home was at Quindrie, South Ronaldsay. He was a volunteer soldier, having joined the colours in Edinburgh on 13th May 1907. Before enlisting he worked as a railwayman.

He remained in the United Kingdom until 25th February 1911 when he went to Egypt. He returned home on 2nd January 1913, where he remained until 2nd November 1915 when the Battalion arrived in France. He was wounded in action in March 1916. He was promoted to Corporal in August 1915 and at the time of his death he was a Lance Sergeant.

The 2nd Battalion relieved the 1st Welsh Guards in the line near Ypres on the 7th April 1916. On the 19th April the Battalion was in the trenches near Wieltze where they were bombarded from 6.00am to 4.45pm. At times the bombardment was intense. It was described by one officer as being the worst they had encountered. Between 8.00pm and 9.00pm a patrol of 50 Germans of the 24th Regiment Bavarian Guard advanced, but when fired on they fled back. Another patrol of 10 men got into the trenches but more than half were killed by a solitary Scots Guard. Eventually the whole of the front line was re-occupied by detached groups of Scots Guards. Several men who had been buried by the shell fire were dug out, some dead and some still alive. Sergeant Thomson must have fallen during this bombardment.

He is now commemorated on Panel 11 of the "Menin Gate" Memorial in Ypres, Belgium.

Company Sergeant Major Magnus S Norquay

491 Company Sergeant Major Magnus Norquay served with No 4 Company, 9th (Glasgow Highlanders) Battalion, Highland Light Infantry, 5th Brigade, 2nd Division.

His home was at Stews and his parents were Magnus and Elizabeth Norquay (née Hossack). He worked as a Law Clerk with MacKenzie Robertson and Co., Writers, Glasgow.

CSM Norquay's long involvement with the army started in Orkney when he joined the Volunteers and later the Territorials in which he served for 24 years. During this time he attended 24 camps. He was with the detachment to London for Queen Victoria's Jubilee, he was at the Royal Review in Edinburgh in 1905 and in 1911 he attended King George V's Coronation in London.

He joined the Battalion in 1896, was promoted to Lance Corporal in 1897, Corporal in 1898, Lance Sergeant in 1899 and Sergeant and Colour Sergeant in 1900. There is no doubt that he was held in the highest esteem by the officers and men of his regiment. He held the Long Service Medal and the Coronation Medal. The 9th Battalion was the first Glasgow Battalion to complete mobilisation and this was done on 5th August 1914. They were in France on 5th November.

CSM Norquay was 45 years old when on the 16th May 1915

he was killed in action. At 8.00pm on that day the Battalion marched out of Richeburg, crossed the Rue du Bois and entered into communication trenches, their task being to make good the line of the Festubert-La Tourelle Road. Each man carried two days' rations and an extra bandoleer of ammunition. They occupied the trenches along with the Worcesters, coming under heavy rifle and machine-gun fire during the morning of the 16th and it appears that CSM Norquay fell at this time.

There was also heavy shelling by both sides all day, making infantry attack impossible. The stretcher-bearers were kept busy carrying back the wounded. The whole area was continually under fire. The 5th Brigade suffered many casualties from the shelling, machine-gun fire and rifle fire. Many wounded men had to be left lying out in no-man's-land all day. Any attempt at rescue had to wait until nightfall. A head shown above the parapet drew immediate fire from the enemy.

A fellow NCO stated " *We lost anything up to 30 killed that day, but above them all stood out the loss which the regiment had received in CSM Norquay. He was esteemed by officers, sergeants and men alike, and was admitted by all to be the father of the regiment. Speaking for the sergeants, there is a blank now in their ranks which will take some time to fill.* "

Another NCO wrote that *"Norquay died a hero and was brave to the finish and was liked by one and all."*

He is commemorated on Panel 37 or 38 at Le Touret Memorial in France.

During the Great War, 598 officers and 9428 other ranks of the Highland Light Infantry lost their lives.

Private William Duncan

36719 Private William Duncan served with 25th (Tyneside Irish) Battalion Northumberland Fusiliers, 102nd Brigade, 34th Division. He enlisted at Fort George in the R.A.S.C. but was transferred to the Northumberland Fusiliers.

His parents were John and Margaret Duncan of Cleat. Before enlisting he was employed as a baker with John Scott, Baker, St Margaret's Hope. He was born on 30th December 1896.

He lost his life on 21st March 1918 when his Battalion was on active service in the Ervillers - Ablainzeville area. At 4.30am on the 21st March a heavy enemy bombardment opened up and continued for about 4 hours. The shells used by the Germans were high explosive along with many gas shells. There was a lull of about 20 minutes followed by another barrage which continued until 11.30am.

When the German "Michael" offensive started on 21st March, the 34th Division was in the centre of the Third Army's VI Corps. The 102nd Brigade was almost overwhelmed with its three Northumberland Fusiliers Battalion HQ's being captured. A shell burst near Private Duncan and he was hit in the chest by a piece of shrapnel. He later died of his wounds. He had been home on leave only three weeks before his death. The war Diary of the 34th Division contained the following sad entry regarding the fate of the Northumberland Fusiliers on the 21st March 1918.

"Message 9.5 p.m. by telephone from 101st Infantry Brigade: Assistant Adjutant 22nd Northumberland Fusiliers says Colonel Acklon killed. Two Battalion HQ's captured. Apart from a few stragglers, none of 22nd left. Two other battalions cut off. Three companies of 25th Northumberland Fusiliers made a counter-attack; not heard of since."

He is commemorated on bay 2 or 3 of the Arras Memorial which is in the Faubourg-d'Amiens Cemetery.

Lance Corporal Archibald Sinclair

106149 Lance Corporal Archibald Sinclair served with the 219th Company Machine Gun Corps, 32nd Division. His parents were James and Isabella Sinclair (née MacKenzie) of Myres, Grimness, and before enlisting he worked at Grutha as a farm servant. He was born on 21st December 1893.

Archibald Sinclair joined the Seaforth Highlanders as many local men did, but was later transferred to the Machine Gun Corps.

On the 1st October 1918 his company was supporting men of the Royal Scots in the capture of the French villages Sequehart and Levingus. The attack was mounted at 4pm, preceded by a heavy barrage by British artillery to keep the enemy quiet. The attack succeeded but the enemy counter-attacked and retook Sequehart. The British fell back about 400 yards. The Royal Scots asked for the barrage which opened up before they were all back. The men of the Machine Gun Corps made their way through exploding British shells, but L/Cpl Sinclair was hit and badly wounded. After the action a search was made for him but he could not be found. It was assumed that the Germans had taken him to their own lines. His mother received the following letter from one of his officers:

I very much regret to have to inform you that your son, Lance Corporal A Sinclair was killed in action on the 1st inst. He was taking part in an attack on a village which was successful, but the enemy counter-attacked and in the counter-attack your son was struck by a piece of shell and died soon after. He was an old member of the Company and a very fine soldier, extremely popular with his comrades. On behalf of the Officers and men of the Company, I convey to you our sincere sympathy in your loss. I can only hope that the knowledge that your son died doing his duty for his country may help to assuage your grief.

After the end of the war his family also received a letter from one of his comrades, explaining in more detail the circumstances of his death. Lance Corporal Sinclair now lies in Grave 9, Row B, Plot 5 of Busigny Communal Cemetery Extension which lies 10 kilometres south west of Le Cateau, Nord, France.

Private Richard Spence

100955 Private Richard Spence served with the 7th Squadron, Machine Gun Corps (Cavalry) attached to the 4th (Royal Irish) Dragoon Guards, 2nd Cavalry Brigade, 1st Cavalry Division. His parents were John and Jane Spence (née Tulloch) of West End, St Margaret's Hope, where his father had a General Merchant's business. He had served an apprenticeship as a baker. He was born on 14th June 1898.

When he enlisted his service number was 22537 and he was with the 6th Reserve Regiment of Cavalry which was a training unit.

The 1st Cavalry Division took part in the Autumn Offensive of 1918 against the Hindenburg Line. The offensive began on the 8th August 1918 with the Battle of Amiens and this was the turning point of the war on the Western Front. The German General Ludendorf described it as the "blackest day of the German army in the history of war".

The Australian and Canadian Corps were supported by the British Cavalry in attacking the first line which ran from Villers - Bretonneux on the Amiens road southwards to Moreuil on the river Avre. By October the Cavalry Brigades had broken through the Hindenburg Line and advanced north west of the Mons-Lissines Line.

Private Richard Spence died in a military hospital on the 12th October 1918 from wounds received near the River Selle. The following letter was received by his parents at the time of his death.

Dear Mr. Spence,
I am exceedingly grieved to have to write to you under these most unhappy circumstances. You have already heard of your son Richard's death but I thought as I was his Section Sergeant you might like to hear from me as I was with him until he was taken to the dressing station where he died the following day, 11th October. Up to the time till he was carried away he was most cheerful, and told his pals not to worry. "I am going to Heaven; trust in the Lord and all will be well," were his words. A braver and cleaner living man I have never met, and he was never happy unless doing something to help his chums in the Section. We have received two parcels and have opened and distributed the contents amongst the section which is the usual custom with us under such circumstances. The whole Section join with me in expressing their deepest sympathy in your bereavement.
Yours very sincerely, F W Cottes, Sgt.

The Machine Gun Corps was raised in 1915 and was composed of Infantry, Cavalry, Heavy and Motor Battalions. The Motor Battalion formed the Tank Corps. The Corps' principal role was to lay down suppressive fire from massed guns to stop the enemy from advancing. It was disbanded in 1922 and the guns were returned to infantry regiments.

Private Richard Spence is interred in Grave 29, Row C, Plot 13, Rocquigny Cemetery near Mamamcourt.

Gunner William C Bruce

368174 Gunner William C Bruce served with the 15th Heavy Battery XXth Heavy Brigade of the Royal Garrison Artillery. His parents were William and Sara Bruce (née. Calder) of Lythes, East Side, and he was born on 23rd October 1897.

On 30th June 1915 the 15th Heavy Battery left Devonport bound for the Dardanelles. The Battery consisted of 6 officers, 199 other ranks, 141 horses, 25 vehicles and 4 sixty pounders. It arrived at the Dardanelles on 10th August 1915 and was in position at Charak Chesma. The Battery returned to Egypt on 9th February 1916.

During 1916 the 15th Heavy Battery was deployed at various positions along the Suez Canal such as El Ferdan, Shaluffa West and Romani. At the end of 1916 it was at Mazar along the railway line to Gaza. The 15th Heavy Battery took part in the first Battle of Gaza on 26th March 1917 and the second Battle of Gaza in April. On 24th November it was north of the Jaffa-Jerusalem road near El Kubri.

During 1918 the Battery was some 20 miles north of the Jaffa-Jerusalem road where it remained until September. It then marched to Beirut, arriving there on 11th October. The Battery then moved south to Surafend via Haifa, arriving there on 4th December. Apparently Gunner William Bruce was left behind at Beirut where he died of pneumonia on 29th October 1918.

The 15th Heavy Battery was disbanded at Ismalia on 31st May 1919.

Gunner William C Bruce was buried in Grave 17, British War Cemetery, Beirut.

Gunner James Sutherland

368147 Gunner James Sutherland served with the 300th Siege Battery, 96th Heavy Artillery Brigade, Royal Garrison Artillery.

His parents were Malcolm and Jessie Sutherland (née. Spence) of Back Road, St Margaret's Hope, and James Sutherland was born on 21st December 1877. He was a brother of Private Robert Sutherland of the Canadian Expeditionary Force (number 22 on the list.)

The 300th Siege Battery was formed at Harwich on 1st November 1916 with the 6 inch and 8 inch Howitzers. After a period of training at Aldershot and Hilsea, the Battery embarked at Folkestone on 16th May 1917 for Le Havre. It moved by rail to Marseilles, arriving at Alexandria on 11th June when it joined the 96th Heavy Artillery Brigade.

The Battery's first action was on 28th June 1917 at Deir-El-Belah, Palestine, and then on the 25th and 26th July, the 8 inch Howitzers bombarded The Maze and Outpost Hill.

The 6 inch Howitzers cooperated with the 52nd Division Artillery in a bombardment of Wadi on 4th September and again on 17th and 18th September at Goetz Redoubt and Tank Ridge. The Battery returned to Goetz with 292 Siege Battery on the 29th October when 58 rounds were fired.

On the 29th April 1918 the Battery was in action at Rentis, 7 miles northeast of Ludd. On 6th August the Gunners supported a British raid on Maxim Hill and Mogg Ridge.

On the 31st October an armistice with Turkey was agreed to take effect at 12 noon, and the Battery's active service ended. The Brigade finished the war in a camp between Ismalia and the Suez Canal.

Sadly, after having survived the war, Gunner James Sutherland died in Egypt on 31st December 1918. He was buried in Grave 169, Beirut War Cemetery, which is located 11 kilometres from the centre of Beirut.

Corporal James Dunnett

107669 Corporal James Dunnett served with the 285 Army Troops Company of the Royal Engineers in Italy.

His parents were James Johnston and Mary Dunnett of Cletts, East Side, South Ronaldsay. He was born on 17th September 1892. His trade was cabinet maker and he also worked for Mr. D. B. Peace, Electric Theatre, Kirkwall. Sadly, after surviving the war Corporal Dunnett died in hospital from influenza on 25th November 1918 during a great pandemic which swept much of the world in 1918 and 1919.

By the time the pandemic had run its course, it had claimed many more lives than had been lost during the war. The total number of lives lost will never be known, but a conservative estimate put the total at 27,000,000. It was considered that India was hit more severely than any other part of the world. By December 1918 at least 5,000,000 had died from influenza. As one observer reported *"It came like a thief in the night, and like a thief it was no respecter of persons. The young, the old, the rich, the poor, all were infected with little warning and with an equally slim chance of recovery. Quacks and charlatans abounded and official medical advice was little more effective."*

In a letter to his mother the Captain of Corporal Dunnett's Company writes *"I am extremely sorry to lose him. By his unfailing cheerfulness and good fellowship, Corporal Dunnett has made himself a great favourite among his comrades, and the company, as one man, received the news of his death with the keenest regret. He served his King and country loyally to the end."*

The 285 Army Troops Company had been engaged in bridge repair and bridge building and on 1st November 1918 towards the end of the Vittorio Veneto battle they built an Inglis steel bridge at Sacile. The allied victory there led to a collapse of the Austrian army with Italian reinforcements advancing rapidly. By the 3rd of November the war on the Italian front had ended. He was interred in Grave No 934, Montecchio Precalcino Com. Cemetery, Vicenza, Italy.

Rifleman Donald S Norquay

29061 Rifleman Donald S. Norquay served with the 2nd Battalion of the 3rd New Zealand Rifle Brigade, New Zealand Division.

His parents were George and Margaret Norquay (née Smith) of Quindrie, South Ronaldsay. Before emigrating to New Zealand, he worked at Bankburn Farm. He was 35 years old at the time of his death. He worked as a labourer in New Zealand before joining the Army.

Donald Norquay joined the New Zealand Expeditionary Force at Trentham Camp on 29th June 1916 and, after a period of training, he embarked for France on 16th October 1916. At that time he was with the 5th Reserve Battalion 3rd New Zealand Rifle Brigade but on arrival in France he was posted to A Company 2nd Battalion on 7th April 1917. He did not have a long period of service on the battlefield, on 12th May he received a gun shot wound to the chest and was admitted to No 1 New Zealand Field Ambulance. On 19th May he was transferred to No 3 Canadian General Hospital, Boulogne, where he died on 21st June 1917.

In the period before his death, the II Anzac Corps were given as their objective the village of Messines. The village had been heavily fortified with a strong trench system and a deep wire entanglement. A number of great acts of gallantry were performed with one New Zealand soldier being awarded the Victoria Cross.

Rifleman Norquay now lies in grave 13, Row A, Plot 4, Boulogne Eastern Cemetery, Pas de Calais.

Private John Marwick

46753 Private John Marwick served with the 2nd Otago Battalion, 2nd New Zealand Brigade, New Zealand Division.

His parents were John and Mary Marwick (née Mitchell). Before emigrating to New Zealand, his home was at Serrigar and he was a farm worker in Longhope. At the time of his death he was aged 27 years.

He left home in 1912 bound for Australia. He spent some time working in the gold fields but found conditions there a bit rough. New Zealand seemed a better prospect. The war started shortly after he arrived there. New Zealand was his new home but the old country was in need of every man she could get to man the trenches of France and Flanders. John Marwick volunteered for service with the New Zealand Expeditionary Force where he served with the 2nd Otago Battalion.

After training he spent some time in Egypt and was then transferred to France where he served for three years unscathed.

On the 5th November 1918, the 2nd New Zealand Brigade relieved the 1st New Zealand Brigade. Little opposition was encountered in their advance through the Mormal Forest, but the state of the forest tracks and machine guns hidden in some of the many shell craters held up the advancing infantry. Private Marwick lost his life during the last action fought by his Division during the last week of the war. The enemy had been driven back a few miles but made a stand at a forester's house where six roads meet. It was there that Private Marwick was hit by a bullet and was killed instantly. He and eight others are buried there.

The following letter from the Battalion Chaplain was received by his brother

I am sending this note to give you the sad news of the death of your brother, 46753 Pte John Marwick of this Battalion. It was during our advance through the famous Mormal Forest. The enemy had been driven back some miles but at a place in the forest where six roads meet, at a forester's house, he made a determined stand. It was during the fighting there that your brother was hit by a bullet and instantly killed. He would not have suffered any pain. His body was carried out and I buried it with eight others where the six roads meet. The place has been marked and registered. We are putting up a permanent cross on Monday. Will you please accept our sympathy in this the day of your loss. We know that it is in the quiet of the homes from which these fine men come that the true price of war is being paid. No one outside the home can ever fully understand what it means when the circle is broken, and the call comes to one whom you have loved to pass through the thin film, which we call death, into the larger life. May God who gave His Son in a great cause bless and strengthen you and yours in the giving of your loved one.

During the war casualties suffered by the New Zealand Expeditionary Force totalled 16,645 killed, 41,317 wounded and 530 taken prisoner.

Private John Marwick now lies in Grave 9, Row A, Plot 2 of Cross Roads Cemetery, 1½ kilometres west of Fontaine-a-Bois Village, France.

Private Robert Sutherland

A38071 Private Robert Sutherland served with the 8th (90th Rifles of Winnipeg) Battalion, 2nd Canadian Brigade, 1st Canadian Infantry Division. He was born on the 23rd December 1896.

Before emigrating to Canada his home was at Back Road, St Margaret's Hope and his parents were Malcolm and Jessie Sutherland (née Spence). He served his time as a baker with James Hunter, Baker, St Margaret's Hope. Before joining the Canadian Army he worked as a labourer. Like many young men at that time he was keen to join the army and get to grips with the enemy. It was thought that the war could not go on for long. He knew that, being only 17 years of age at the time, he would not be accepted by the Canadian Army. When he enlisted he gave his date of birth as 29th November 1892. He was a brother of Gunner James Sutherland who is number 18 on the list.

He joined the Canadian Army at Port Arthur on the 19th December 1914 when only 17 years old. On 3rd of August 1915 he was transferred to the 8th Battalion in France.

Private Sutherland lost his life midway through the Battle of the Somme and was the only local soldier to fall in that terrible battle. He was 19 years old at the time. An item in the Orcadian at the time of his death stated *"Much sympathy is felt for his mother and other relatives in their loss. All who knew him are sure that among all the gallant Canadians who have answered the Motherland's call there was no finer fellow and no more fearless soldier than Bob Sutherland".*

From the 10th September 1916 onwards, the 8th Battalion was in reserve, sometimes providing 100 men on trench maintenance and again 30 men as a Burying Party. At 3.30 p.m. on the 25th September the Battalion paraded, ready to take up position in the trenches to the left of Courcelette. The Battalion numbered 644 other ranks and 23 officers. Preserved rations for 2 days were issued to all men. The 8th Battalion relieved the 7th in the trenches and suffered 10 casualties in the move to the front line.

By 1.30 am on the 26th September all troops were reported to be in their jumping off positions. The Battalion advanced under an intense bombardment of the enemy forward positions and were soon reported to have captured Zollern Trench and 3 officers and 80 other ranks had advanced to Hessian trench. The number of unwounded prisoners captured by the 8th Battalion amounted to 160, most of whom surrendered very readily.

At 2 pm on the 27th the Battalion received orders that they were to be relieved by another Canadian unit. Casualties suffered by the 8th Battalion in this action on the Somme came to 13 officers and 446 other ranks killed, wounded or missing. At some time on the 28th September, Private Sutherland received a gun shot wound to his right thigh which was not thought to be serious, but blood poisoning set in and his condition rapidly deteriorated. He died at No 2 General Hospital, Le Havre on the 30th.

He was interred in Grave 7, Row H, Division 3 of the Ste Marie Cemetery, Le Havre, France.

The 8th Battalion had a nick-name 'The Little Black Devils'. This was earned on 23rd April 1885 at the Battle of Fish Creek. The Battalion had been sent to quell the Metis rebellion led by Louis Reil who had extended his campaign to cover the entire Northwest Territories of Canada. The rebels were surprised at the cool, steady advance of the Battalion and prisoners were later heard to say "The Redcoats we know but who are those Little Black Devils?". At that time the Battalion's uniform was dark green in colour.

Private Gilbert O Thomson

8584 Private Gilbert O. Thomson served with the 2nd (Eastern Ontario) Battalion, 1st Canadian Brigade, 1st Canadian Infantry Division

His parents were Gilbert and Margaret Thomson (née Gilmour) of Academy, South Parish, South Ronaldsay. His father was a lighthouse keeper who had served on the Pentland Skerries but at the time of Gilbert's birth, was at Port Charlotte, Kilchoman, Islay.

Before emigrating to Canada he had served as a Territorial soldier with the 5th Battalion, Royal Scots Fusiliers. When in Canada he worked as a teamster.

He volunteered for service with the Canadian Army on 22nd September 1914 and on 3rd October 1914 he embarked on the SS Cassandra bound for Plymouth. They landed there on the 14th October and proceeded to Salisbury Plain for training. The First Canadian Contingent consisted of 17,873 officers and men with 4,943 horses. After a period of training, they embarked at Avonmouth for St Nazaire in February 1915.

On 3rd March they took over the Armentières section of the line. In every soldiers' paybook was a message from Field-Marshal Lord Kitchener which stated "You have to perform a task which will need your courage, your energy and your patience".

From the 7th to 20th April 1915, the Battalion was in reserve at Winnezeele and on the 21st marched to Valmertinghe, about three miles west of Ypres in Second Army reserve.

Private Gilbert Thomson lost his life on the first day of the Second Battle of Ypres. Thursday 22nd April 1915 was a fine spring day with the Canadians holding the front line between the Ypres - Poelcappelle road and the Gavenstafel - Passchendaele road. They could not have known that by the weekend, 2000 of their comrades would be dead.

The 2nd Eastern Ontario and the 3rd Toronto Battalions went into the front line to reinforce the 10th and 16th Battalions south of Kitchener's Wood. At 5pm on the 22nd April a large cloud of poison gas could be seen approaching the Canadian positions. The French troops in the area fled, leaving the Canadians to deal with the threat as well as they could. The gas was quickly followed by the German Infantry which poured into the gap. The Canadians had a heavy price to pay during their time in Flanders.

Gilbert Thomson has no known grave. He is commemorated on Panel 10 of the Ypres (Menin Gate) Memorial.

Private William R Cromarty

1695190 Private William R Cromarty served with the Headquarters Troop 77th (Statue of Liberty) Division, American Expeditionary Force. His parents were Samuel and Elizabeth Cromarty (née Ridland) of South Cara, Grimness, South Ronaldsay.

He served an apprenticeship as a tailor before emigrating to the United States and made his home at Liberty, New York where he worked in his uncle's business.

When America declared war against Germany he volunteered for service with the American Army. After only three weeks training with the 306th Infantry Regiment at Camp Upton, he was transferred to the Headquarters Troop of the 77th Division which sailed for Liverpool on 27th March 1918. The Division landed on 12th May and were in Calais on the 13th. A period of training followed with British Officers and NCO's.

The inexperienced soldiers of the 77th Division entrained for the Baccarat section of the front line on 6th June, and the 77th was the first American Division to see action. At 4am on the 24th June, they were on the receiving end of 3000 rounds of Phosgene and Mustard gas shells when the enemy bombarded the sector held by them. Casualties were reported to be light, mostly due to removing gas masks too soon. The division was relieved by the 37th American Division on the 4th August.

By mid August the 77th were back in the front line in the Valley of Vesle, where both sides were engaged in attacks and raids with artillery of both sides constantly shelling forward and rear areas.

On the 4th September the 77th Division crossed the river Vesle and captured Bazoches, and by the 6th they had advanced 9 kilometres to reach the south bank of the river Aisne where the front line was established.

On the 16th September the 77th Division was relieved by an Italian division. During the operations at the river Vesle and the subsequent advance, the 77th Division lost nearly 4800 men.

On the 11th, Private Cromarty was driving officers of the 370th Infantry to 77th Division Headquarters when the vehicle received a direct hit by a high explosive shell. All the occupants of the vehicle were killed instantly.

Private William Cromarty now lies in Plot D, Row 7, Grave 3, Oise-Aisne American Cemetery, Fere-en-Tardenous (Aisne), France.

Private William R Cromarty

Deckhand John Brown

19268 Deckhand John Brown served with Royal Naval Reserve (Trawlers) on HMT Prefect

He was married to Margaret Jane Norquay and had two sons and two daughters, Hector, John, Catherine and Dorothy. His home was at Ferryhouse, Grimness, South Ronaldsay. He was born on 27th August 1879.

Before joining the Royal Navy he worked as a rural postman. His parents were James and Jane Brown (née Fraser) also of Ferryhouse.

On the 13th August 1918 his ship was berthed at the King William Dock, Dundee. During the evening a cry for help was heard and John Brown lost his life by drowning while trying to save the life of someone in trouble.

He was interred in the Eastern Cemetery, Dundee.

The trawlers were the workhorses of the Navy and had many and varied tasks. They were employed on convoy escort duties, the protection of fishing vessels, the detection of enemy submarines and had many uses in Naval Bases and dockyards.

Deckhand John Brown.

Deckhand John G. H. Thomson

Deckhand John G. H. Thomson served with the Royal Naval Mercantile Marine Reserve

He was born at Newark, Sanday on 3rd June 1887 but at the time of his death his home was at Blanster, St Margaret's Hope. His parents were William D. S. and Jessie J. Thomson (née Budge).

After leaving school, he trained as a blacksmith with Donald Mowat in the South Parish. In 1911 he trained as a lightkeeper at Noss Head and also served at Dunnett Head and was at the Pentland Skerries in 1913.

On the night of 15th August 1916 he was on night watch on his ship the War Department Drifter, Davda, when he must have slipped and he fell overboard. He was not reported missing until the following morning.

At the time of the accident the Davda was on station at the Hoxa Boom, part of the anti-submarine defences of Scapa Flow. The body was recovered on the following evening and the funeral which was attended by locals and fellow crewmen took place from Blanster to the South churchyard.

He is pictured overleaf in the uniform of the Northern Lighthouse Board.

Deckhand John G H Thomson.

Engineer John Simpson

121274 Engineer John Simpson served with His Majesty's Transport Service. His parents were John and Helen Simpson (née Wade) and his home was at West End, St Margaret's Hope where his father kept a Seed and General Merchant's business. He was born on 9th January 1890.

John Simpson served as Third Engineer on the Clan MacPherson, a ship of 4779 gross tons, built in 1905 by Richardson Westgarth & Co of West Hartlepool. The Clan MacPherson was requisitioned by the Government on 15th March 1915 and from that date onwards she was only employed on Government work. She made several voyages to Alexandria with military stores and also played her part in the Gallipoli Campaign, landing troops and guns at Suvla Bay. Most of her voyages were between the United Kingdom and the Middle East with the occasional trip to the Far East and to America.

Her last voyage was from Gibraltar to Boston, Massachusetts and Portland in Maine for a cargo of grain and flour for Malta. The return trip was safely made and the cargo was unloaded. She then left Malta for Bizerta in Tunisia where, on the 4th March 1918, she joined a convoy bound for Colon. The night of the 4th was stormy and very dark and about 10 o'clock, when 24 miles north of Cape Serrat, the Clan MacPherson was torpedoed by the German submarine UC27.

The Master, Captain Mee, immediately ordered all lifeboats away, an order which was difficult to carry out because of the heavy seas. The last boat to come alongside was wrecked by the falling foremast and 18 men were lost. The Master and the Fourth Officer were the last to leave the stricken ship, and after spending two hours in the water, were rescued and landed at Bizerta. John Simpson was among the many who did not return. The Clan Line lost 28 ships during the Great War with 8 sunk in 1918.

Engineer John Simpson is commemorated on Panel 5 of the Tower Hill Memorial in London.

**Photo of Able Seaman William
Sissons, sole survivor of the Opal**

HMS Narborough and HMS Opal

1918, the last year of the war, had a disastrous start in South
Ronaldsay. The year began with a brilliant display of the Aurora
Borealis. This is usually a sure sign of bad weather to come,
and this was certainly what happened. What followed was
reported in The Orkney Herald as being the worst snowstorm
for 50 years. The first snow fell on Sunday 6th January and it
continued to snow on and off, accompanied by severe gale
force winds, until Saturday the 19th January when a thaw set
in.

It was into weather conditions like this that the two M Class
destroyers HMS Opal (Lieutenant Commander Charles Malan)
and HMS Narborough (Lieutenant Edmond M Bowly) with
the light cruiser HMS Boadicea left Scapa Flow at 0830hrs on
the 12th January on a Dark Night Patrol (DNP). As that name
suggests these patrols were carried out on moonless nights in
an attempt to stop mine laying in the approaches to naval bases
by fast enemy warships. DNPs were carried out by one light
cruiser and two destroyers. When the ships left Scapa Flow the
weather conditions were reported to be good with the wind
force 1 and the glass fine but steady. By 1828hrs, the two
destroyers were caught in a severe blizzard with a rapidly rising
sea and, finding it difficult to navigate with visibility reduced
almost to nil, were ordered to return to Scapa Flow. At 1840hrs
Opal asked for the lights on Copinsay, Pentland Skerries, Noss
Head, Stroma, Swona and Cantick Head and later requested

fog signals because of "blinding snow". HMS Narborough reported that gear on her forecastle was being carried away by the sea and the last message to come from HMS Opal enabled the Wireless Station at Old Head, South Ronaldsay to get a fix on her position of 195° True. At 2127 hrs the incomplete signal was received: *"Urgent. Have run aground."* The very bad visibility coupled with an error in navigation by the Captain of the Opal resulted in the loss of HMS Opal and HMS Narborough. Both ships drove ashore on the Clett of Crura in Windwick Bay, and 187 seamen from both ships went to their deaths in the wild and cruel seas of the bay.

There was only one survivor, Able Seaman William Sissons of HMS Opal. He was found sheltering on a ledge on the cliff in the snow on the morning of the 14th January. He had been at his post at No 2 gun between Opal's 2nd and 3rd funnels, and when the ship began to break up, he climbed on to one of the funnels where he was able to get some warmth. When the funnel began to collapse, he swam about 100 yards to the shore and was able to climb some way up the cliff. He was to spend 36 hours on the shore and on the cliff before being rescued by a boat from the trawler Michael Malony which made its way through rocks and wreckage to the shore. He was then transferred to HMS Peyton and later to the hospital ship China where he made a full recovery from the hardships he had endured. It was reported that he was able to semaphore the name of his ship to his rescuers. After he had recovered he was interviewed on board China. He stated that the weather was very bad with a heavy stern sea. He reckoned that Opal's speed was 7 knots when she ran up on to the rocks. Three blasts were given on the siren and the order to "Abandon Ship" was given. The three blasts were repeated by Narborough. The Captain of Opal and a Sub-Lieutenant were on the bridge at the time. It was thought that more lives could have been saved if the men had been able to scale the cliffs but this was not possible in the weather conditions at that time. Local boats could not be launched in the very rough seas to go to their aid because of weather conditions, and a search for the missing warships could not be undertaken until the morning of the 13th when 4 sloops with trawlers, drifters and shore parties joined in. The wrecks were eventually discovered by HMS Peyton on the 14th.

About a week later, during the night, there was a terrific explosion which sent parts of the ships and ammunition on to the cliff tops. During the previous day a torpedo was seen surging around in the surf below. HMS Boadicea returned safely to Scapa Flow.

An enquiry into the loss of the two warships was held on board HMS Colossus on 17th January 1918, and part of the findings of the enquiry stated *"Vessels were lost owing to an error on the part of the Captain of the Opal, but the situation was peculiar and difficult, and the error human, although an officer of greater experience would probably not have committed it."*

There is a discrepancy regarding the exact number of men lost on the two warships. The records of the Commonwealth War Graves Commission show a total of 187 and the Ministry of Defence 188. A total of 96 casualties have been positively identified from HMS Opal and 91 from HMS Narborough, so 187 would appear to be the correct total.

Both Opal and Narborough were in action during the Battle of Jutland on 31st May 1916, and both ships survived. HMS Opal was with the 12th Flotilla attached to Admiral Sir John Jellicoe's Battle Fleet, and HMS Narborough was with the 13th Flotilla, attached to Vice Admiral Sir David Beatty's Battle Cruiser Fleet. M Class Destroyers had a speed of 34 knots and were armed with three single 4 inch Quick Firing guns, two 2-pounder anti-aircraft guns and four 21 inch torpedo tubes.

The 187 seamen who were lost were remembered by the Royal Navy when a wreath was cast into the waters of Windwick Bay on the 14th October 1993 from HMS Orkney. On the following Sunday a commemorative service was held at the Windwick Bay viewpoint and a memorial was dedicated to the men of the two warships by Brigadier Malcolm G Dennison, the Lord Lieutenant of Orkney.

H.M.S. Opal full speed ahead at Jutland. – Negative Number SP2017

H.M.S. Narborough. – Negative Number SP1425

The Second World War

On the 3rd of September 1939 Britain found itself once again at war with Germany. This time it was not to be a war of stalemate with the armies bogged down in the trenches of France and Flanders. This war was to be fought on land, sea and in the air with the civilian population at risk along with the armed forces. Many of the cities were heavily bombed with thousands of lives being lost.

During the war years the population of South Ronaldsay must have doubled with the influx of servicemen. There was a radar station on the Ward Hill, three coastal batteries (two at Hoxa Head and one at Grimness), three anti-aircraft batteries (two at Hoxa and one at Herston), a military hospital with dental clinic, a detention barracks, no less than eighteen searchlights and several other camps. The Royal Navy had a mine depot at the Pier where they serviced the Hoxa Sound Minefield.

During the early years of the war, air raids were frequent with reconnaissance and photographic sorties by single aircraft becoming a common occurrence. South Ronaldsay was bombed and landmines fell on several occasions.

It was after one of these air-raids that the only civilian fatality occurred. Margaret Berston from Wheems was out working in the fields when she was hit by shrapnel. She died in hospital on 20th March 1942 as a result of wounds received. She left a five year old boy, Dennis.

During an earlier raid on the night 10th / 11th April 1940, two Gunners of the Royal Artillery were killed when a shell exploded in the breech of the gun at the Herston Anti-Aircraft battery (178 Battery, 63AA Regiment, Royal Artillery). Gunners Thomas Cockburn and Alfred Sayers both lie in the North Churchyard where their graves are marked with Commonwealth War Graves head stones.

On 7th May 1945, Germany surrendered unconditionally and 8th and 9th May were National holidays. Again after the 14th August when the Japanese Emperor broadcast surrender, the 15th and 16th were National holidays.

As in 1918, the servicemen and women returned to take up their civilian occupations again. The war had taken six years off the lives of some of the men but it had taken life itself from ten local men. Two soldiers, two Royal Navy men, one airman and five Merchant Seamen did not return.

At a Service on Sunday 11th May 1947 in St Margaret's Church tokens of remembrance were presented to relatives of the fallen.

On Friday 9th May a "Welcome Home" social evening was held in the Cromarty Hall when Scrolls and gifts were presented to 103 ex-service men and women.

The ten brave men who did not return from the war are

commemorated on the plaque which was unveiled on Sunday 5th September 1948 by Miss Marjory Rosie of Roselea. She had lost her uncle on 2nd January 1942 when serving on a Russian convoy. The short service was conducted by Rev. J. C. Steen of St Peters and Rev. D. S. MacAlpine in the presence of a large gathering.

Margaret Berston.

Photo of Military Funeral of Gunners Thomas Cockburn & Alfred Sayers of 178 Battery

Private John S Doull

14742203 Private John S Doull served with No 2 Platoon No 3 Company Gordon Highlanders

His parents were Benjamin and Agnes Doull (née Scott) of Church Road, St Margaret's Hope. He was born on 4th January 1924. Before joining the army he worked in the family business as a van man.

While training as an infantry soldier at Bridge of Don Barracks, Aberdeen he became ill and died on 21st March 1945 in Old Mill Hospital, Aberdeen.

He was buried in the North Churchyard, South Ronaldsay.

Seaman John M Gunn

PX20991A Seaman John M Gunn served with the Royal Naval Reserve on HMS Cape Howe, also known as the Prunella. His parents were John and Mary Gunn (née Annal) of Blinkbonny, Herston, South Ronaldsay. He was born on the 10th December 1919. After leaving school he served an apprenticeship as a joiner with W A Sinclair of St Margaret's Hope, and later went to work at Lyness Naval Base where he worked for Baldrays, a company constructing underground oil storage tanks in the Hoy Hills.

After joining the Royal Navy, he was drafted to HMS Cape Howe, a ship of 4443 tons, built in 1930 by Lithgows of Port Glasgow for Pardoe-Thomas of Newport, Monmouthshire. The Cape Howe was a cargo ship but on the 15th September 1939 she was requisitioned by the Admiralty, and was commissioned as a Special Service Vessel (Decoy Ship) or, as they were well known in the First World War, a Q Ship.

A total of ten merchant ships were converted to Special Service Vessels including Cape Howe's sister ship, Cape Sable. During WWI the Q Ships had considerable success but this was not reflected during the Second World War. The role of the ships was to lure the U-boats to the surface where they could be attacked by gunfire.

The ships were fitted with buoyancy material and, depending

on size, armed with four or more concealed 4 inch or 5.9 inch guns, two or more 21 inch torpedo tubes and depth charges. To the U-boat commanders they appeared to be genuine merchant ships going about their lawful business and not worth using a torpedo on. It was hoped that the U-boat would surface to attack the ship with gunfire and the ship's armaments would be revealed.

The Special Service Vessels had no success during the final months of 1939 nor during 1940, and their use ended early in 1941. This released a large number of highly trained seamen for service elsewhere in the Royal Navy. The U-boat commanders had been ordered not to surface but to use torpedoes and consequently the ships were unable to retaliate.

On the 21st June 1940, no fewer than eight U-boats were operating in the south west approaches to the English Channel when HMS Cape Howe was sighted and attacked and sunk by the U28 (Kapitan Leutnant Gunter Kuhnke, Knight's Cross).

The Cape Howe was reported to have remained afloat for four hours after the attack, enabling 13 survivors to leave the stricken ship. Unfortunately Seaman John Gunn was not one of them. The survivors were picked up from a raft 90 miles south west of the Bishops Rock Lighthouse.

The U28 was a type VIIA U-boat, built in 1935 by A G Weber of Bremen, and was commissioned on 12th September 1936.

She sank as a result of a training accident at Neustadt U-boat pier with the loss of one man. The U28 carried out 7 patrols and sank 13 ships with a tonnage of 56272 tons.

Seaman John Gunn is commemorated on Panel 44, Column 1 of the Portsmouth Naval Memorial.

Seaman Magnus L Henderson

Seaman Magnus L Henderson served in the Merchant Navy on MV Empire Statesman, ex Pellice, ex Ansaldo Ottavo.

His parents were William and Jane Henderson (née Eunson) and his home was at East Shaird, South Ronaldsay. He was born on 14th February 1906. Before joining the Merchant Navy, he worked at Thurrigar, South Parish, South Ronaldsay.

The Empire Statesman was a general cargo vessel of 5360 gross tons with a speed of 10 knots. She was built in 1920 by Giorgio Ansaldo & Co of Genoa, Sestri, Italy for the Societa Commerciale Navigazione of Milan.

On the 10th June 1940, Italy entered the war and the ship was immediately seized by the government while she was lying at Newcastle. She was managed by the Runciman Shipping Co of London for the Ministry of War Transport.

Seaman Magnus Henderson lost his life on the 11th December 1940 when his ship was torpedoed by the German submarine U94 (Kapitan Leutnant Herbert Kuppisch.) The Empire Statesman sailed from Freetown on 19th November on a voyage to Oban and then Middlesborough with a general cargo. She reported engine trouble 2 days later but sailed on independently until she was sunk by the U94 when west of Ireland.

The fate of the ship was confirmed on 24th December when the British destroyer HMS Kipling reported that they had recovered the body of the fourth officer from a raft. Lying beside him was a lifebuoy from the Empire Statesman. The medical officer of HMS Kipling estimated that the officer had been dead for about a week. The Empire Statesman carried a crew of 32 seamen and all were lost.

The U94 was sunk off Haiti on the 28th August 1942. She was attacked with depth charges by an American Catalina from VP92 Squadron and was rammed by the Canadian corvette HMCS Oakville. Twenty-six German sailors survived the sinking and 19 were killed. The U94 was a type VIIC U-boat built by Germaniawerft of Kiel and was commissioned on the 10th August 1940. During her war career the U94 sank 25 allied ships with a total of 137395 tons. Seaman Magnus Henderson is commemorated on Panel 45 of the Tower Hill Memorial in London.

Sergeant Robert M Mathieson

628213 Sergeant Robert M Mathieson was an Air-Gunner serving with 106 Squadron, Bomber Command, Royal Air Force

His parents were Donald and Williamina Mathieson (née Muir) of Quoy of Herston, South Ronaldsay. He was born on 14th October 1920. Before joining the Royal Air Force he worked at Waltness, Shapinsay.

106 Squadron was based at Coningsby in Lincolnshire. On 21st July 1942 Lancaster aircraft no. R5576 was tasked with bombing practice. As the bomber was taking off, the port inner engine failed but it gained about 200 feet after a circuit of the aerodrome. It then stalled and struck the ground in a spin to port.

Sadly, the entire crew lost their lives as a result of the accident. A total of ten men were lost including two Canadians and an Australian. Sgt. Mathieson was buried in Grave 1275, Row 65, Coningsby Cemetery, Lincolnshire.

In the weeks before the accident the squadron flew many sorties over Germany attacking the Krupps Works at Essen, Berlin and the Neptune shipyards in the Baltic port of Rostock. They also made periodic visits to the Scharnhorst and Gneisenau before they escaped through the Channel.

On 13th April 1942, 106 Squadron had a new commander. He was Wing-Commander Guy Gibson DSO DFC who was later to be awarded the Victoria Cross for his part in the Dambusters Raid on the Mohne, Eder and Sorpe dams in Germany.

Leading Seaman James Russell

R/JX177410 Leading Seaman James Russell served with the Royal Navy on HMS Baranca.

His parents were John C. and Jessie R. Russell (née Muir) and his home was at Shaird, Sandwick, South Ronaldsay. He was born on 21st June 1917. He worked at home on the farm and went inshore fishing.

In the period before the war started there was work for many at Lyness as the country re-armed and prepared for the war that was sure to come. James Russell went to Lyness in July 1937 and worked for the Government but, as soon as war was declared, many of the civilian workers were drafted into the Royal Navy and he joined H.M.S. Baranca.

H.M.S. Baranca was built by Hall Russell of Aberdeen in 1938. She was designed for laying and maintaining the antisubmarine nets which were laid across the entrances to naval bases and some ports.

On the 24th April 1940 Baranca was on station at the Hoxa Boom and was engaged on maintenance work when James Russell was hit by a cable, which had become loose from the winch and he was knocked into the sea.

A rescue attempt was immediately carried out by the crew of

the ship but sadly, it was in vain. His body was not recovered from the sea.

He is commemorated on panel 38 column 1 of the Portsmouth Naval Memorial.

Second Officer William S Rosie

Second Officer William Rosie served in the Merchant Navy on SS Waziristan. His parents were William and Maggie Jean Rosie (née Sinclair) of Roselea, St Margaret's Hope. He was born on the 28th November 1920.

2nd Officer William Rosie lost his life on the 2nd January 1942 when his ship was bombed and then torpedoed. The SS Waziristan was a ship of 5135 gross tons with a speed of 10 knots. She was built in 1924 by Short Bros. Ltd. of Sunderland for the Hindustan Steam Shipping Co Ltd. and was managed by Common Bros. of Newcastle.

The ship's first encounter with the enemy came on the 6th February 1941 when she was bombed by German aircraft when on a voyage to the west of Shetland. She was disabled by a near miss and was towed to Kirkwall for temporary repairs on the 10th February 1941. In November 1941 the SS Waziristan was lying at Bush Terminal, Brooklyn, New York. Orders were received to load war materials and sail to Murmansk in Northern Russia. She was the first vessel to attempt a voyage from the United States to Murmansk during the war. Her cargo included 1000 tons of copper ingots, tanks for the Russian Army and other armaments.

She arrived at Sydney, Nova Scotia on 27th November 1941 to await the formation of convoy SC60. After a wait of 7 days, along with two other merchant ships and an escort of two armed trawlers, the convoy sailed to Reykjavik to await the arrival of another convoy from the United Kingdom.

Many of the ships in the north-bound convoy had been damaged by adverse weather and it was decided that convoy PQ7A would sail from Hvalfjord on Boxing Day and it would be composed of only 2 ships, the SS Waziristan and the Panamanian registered Cold Harbour with the escorting trawlers Ophelia and Hugh Walpole. On the departure of the trawlers the two merchant ships were due to rendezvous with the minesweepers Britonart and Salamander but they failed to meet and the two ships sailed on unescorted into the teeth of an arctic storm.

The ships soon became separated and without the benefit of radar, contact was not re-established. The last sighting of the Waziristan was at 1600 hours on New Year's Day 1942 when she was seen by the Cold Harbour when she was south-west of Bear Island. The Cold Harbour eventually arrived safely at her destination Iokanka, a port between Murmansk and Archangel on 12th January. Her captain reported that the Waziristan may have been caught in the ice.

The fate of the Waziristan could not be established until after the end of the war when German Military Records became available for research. The naval records and further documents showed that she had been bombed, and the log of U134 (Kapitan Leutnant Rudolf Schendel) indicate the circumstances which led to the loss of the ship and her crew of 37 seamen and 10 gunners.

The U134 was only on her second patrol and in the early morning of the 2nd January 1942 was running on the surface when she sighted the Waziristan steaming along to the south of Bear Island. At 0622 hrs GMT the U134 fired a torpedo from a stern tube which missed. A second torpedo was fired from the bow at 0639hrs and this also missed the target. It was thought that both failures were caused by the effect of the severe cold on the mechanism of the torpedoes. At 0648hrs a third torpedo fired from a bow tube hit the Waziristan amidships from a range of 400m. This caused the ship to break in two and after half an hour she sank some 18 miles south of Bear Island. Two of the ship's lifeboats were seen in the water but no survivors were ever found. The Waziristan was the first ship to be lost in the Russian Convoy Campaign but many more ships and men were to follow her.

The U134 was sunk just after midnight on the 24th August 1943 when she was south-west of Cape Finisterre. She was attacked by Wellington XIV "J" of 179 Squadron, Royal Air Force using a Leigh Light and depth charges. There were no survivors from the crew of 48. The U-boat had sunk two allied ships and one German ship in error. The U-boat was a type VIIC submarine built by Bremer Vulcan and was commissioned on 26th July 1941.

Second Officer William Rosie is commemorated on Panel 117 of the Tower Hill Memorial in London.

During the 1970s the Waziristan became the target of a firm of divers and salvers. Their objective was the 1000 tons of copper ingots which at that time had a value of £750,000. They failed to locate the ship and the project was abandoned. Some time later, the divers moved further into the Arctic and were successful in recovering most of the gold from the wreck of HMS Edinburgh.

Able Seaman Walter Sinclair

Able Seaman Walter Sinclair served in the Merchant Navy on the SS Daxhound.

His parents were Walter and Jane Sinclair (née Learmonth) and his home was at Sorquoy, East Side, South Ronaldsay. He was born on 26th March 1898 at Sorquoy. He worked on the family farm until 1927 when he joined the Merchant Navy remaining until 1939 when he returned to South Ronaldsay to work. He rejoined the Merchant Navy in 1940.

The SS Daxhound was an oil tanker, and on the 11th October 1941 was berthed at the jetty known as the "Hulk" in Skala Fjord, Eysturoy in the Faroe Islands. Walter Sinclair lost his life when a single, low-flying, enemy aircraft strafed the ship. On hearing the gunfire he rushed on deck to assist in the defence of his ship and was caught in a hail of bullets. The Daxhound had been at anchor in the fjord for several days before coming alongside for water.

Skalafjordur had been under attack by the Luftwaffe since 8.30am and at one time five aircraft were reported over the island of Nolsoy. There were several ships lying in the middle of the fjord and no doubt they would have been attractive targets for the enemy. The presence of the SS Daxhound was the cause of concern to the local people. The consequences of a direct hit on a tanker full of petrol when lying alongside the jetty would have been horrendous.

The aircraft came under fire by guns of the 56th LAA Battery, Royal Artillery, and, according to the log of the battery, a total of 96 rounds were fired. Bren and Lewis guns were also used.

Able Seaman Walter Sinclair died on board the hospital boat Reydi Krossur (Red Cross) on his way to the hospital in Torshavn.

He was buried in Grave 120, Torshavn Cemetery in the part reserved for British Servicemen. These graves all lie in the north central part of the cemetery.

Trooper David Sinclair

7951413 Trooper David Sinclair served with C Squadron, 50th Royal Tank Regiment, 23rd Armoured Brigade, 8th Army. His parents were David and Isabella Sinclair (née Matches) of Heads, South Ronaldsay. He was born on the 20th January 1918.

On leaving school he went to work for John Sclater, Draper, in Kirkwall and then for Messrs Harcus, Linklater & Co of Shetland. In the autumn of 1939 he became manager of the Lyness branch of D H Gorn, Draper, Kirkwall.

He joined the Royal Tank Regiment in March 1942, doing his training in England. In October 1942 he was sent to Cairo via South Africa where he received training in desert warfare, ultimately joining the 8th Army in Tunisia for the final stages of the North Africa Campaign. The 50th Royal Tank Regiment took part in heavy fighting in support of the 51st Highland Division and the 5th Indian Infantry Brigade at the battle of Tel-el-Aqqaqir and again at Wadi Akarit in support of the 50th and 51st Divisions.

After the defeat of Rommel's Afrika Korps, the 23rd Armoured Brigade began training for the invasion of Sicily. The 50th Royal Tank Regiment said goodbye to their Valentine tanks and converted to Shermans.

The landings on Sicily took place on 10th July 1943 with the 23rd Armoured Brigade again in support of the 51st Highland Division. The campaign in Sicily was hard fought but short lived, ending on 17th August when the United States 3rd Division entered Messina.

The rocky and scrubby terrain of Sicily was very different from the open desert of Africa where the tanks were able to range freely around the country. In Sicily they were mainly confined to the roads, but it was good training for the invasion of Italy which was to come soon. In the short Sicilian Campaign the 23rd Armoured Brigade lost 25 out of its force of 95 tanks.

The 50th Royal Tank Regiment had been in action continuously since July 1942. They had been with the 8th Army from El Alamein and had a long and bitter fight of almost 4000 miles to reach their present position on the Adriatic coast of Italy. They had fought in Egypt, Libya, Cyrenaica, Tripolitania, Tunisia, Sicily and now Italy. For much of that time they had been in support of the famous 51st Highland Division.

The Italians had signed an armistice on 3rd September 1943 and were no longer a threat to the Allied armies. The enemies were now the Germans of course, and the atrocious winter weather. On the 9th September the 23rd Armoured Brigade landed at Taranto on the Italian mainland and soon faced stiff opposition. They encountered really close country and village fighting in support of the 8th Indian Division.

The Battle of the River Sangro was fought as a battle against nature as well as the Germans. During early November there were days of torrential rain making it almost impossible for the heavy vehicles to go across country. They quickly became bogged down and the roads became almost impassable with craters blown in them. The bridges over the rivers had also been demolished and the approaches to possible crossing points had been heavily mined. A captured German soldier said that they had used every mine they had.

The first attempt at crossing the River Sangro was on the night of the 19th November when most of the tanks were stuck on the river bed. At one period 20 tanks were bogged down with others stuck in the river.

It was not until the afternoon of the 26th November that the River Sangro was crossed. During the Battle of the River Sangro the regiment lost 15 of its tanks including 9 from mines, 2 knocked out by shellfire and 1 lost in the river.

At the end of the Sangro River operations, the following message was received.

" I write to congratulate you and the whole of your Brigade for the wonderful way they have fought during the last battle. I think it is true to say that the success of the Sangro battle was mainly due to the dash and fighting qualities of your Brigade. The difficulties of the country and the going made the task

extremely difficult but they were determined to overcome both. Thank you very much and I envy you your command of which you must be really proud."

On the 14th December the 50th Royal Tank Regiment had crossed the River Moro and were engaged in an attempt to capture a section of the Ortona-Orsogna road with the intention of denying its use to the enemy. By the 18th December the Regiment had advanced and Consalvi had been captured.

Plans were made on the 20th December for C Squadron to support the 5th Battalion Essex Regiment on the 19th Indian Infantry Brigade section. At this time the Regiment had 28 serviceable tanks. In the advance on the 21st December, Trooper Sinclair's tank became bogged down and at this time a number of wounded Indian soldiers could be seen.

The crew of the tank went on foot to try to bring the injured men to safety but in doing so one of the men stepped on a mine. When the medical officer reached them he found that Trooper Sinclair and another man were dead and the tank commander very seriously wounded.

Trooper David Sinclair is interred in Plot 14, Row B, Grave 23, Sangro River Cemetery, Italy.

Captain Andrew Thomson

Captain Andrew Thomson, Master Mariner, served with the Merchant Navy. His ship was the SS Ben Avon.

His parents were William D S and Jessie Jean Thomson (née Budge) of Swanson House, St Margaret's Hope. He was born at Backaskaill, Sanday on 13th September 1896.

Andrew Thomson served his seagoing apprenticeship on the Ben Lawers, a ship of the Ben Line which he joined in 1914. Except for a period of 15 months, he stayed with that line for the remainder of his life.

He obtained his Master's Certificate at the age of 24 years and in 1929 was sailing as Master of the Benvenue. At that time he was the youngest master in the Ben Line.

It was on the 29th August 1940 that the Ben Avon left Penang with a cargo of rubber, jute and hemp, bound for London. She was a fine ship of 5872 gross tons, built in 1930 by Lithgows of Port Glasgow. She was armed with one 5.9 inch gun mounted aft.

The Pinguin was a German surface raider disguised as a Norwegian freighter. She was armed with six 5.9 inch guns and an Arado seaplane. She sailed from Germany on 15th June 1940 with 300 mines for her own use and 25 torpedoes and 50 mines for transfer to U-boats in mid-ocean. She was commanded by Captain Kruder, an officer who was said to be of the old school. He had served with distinction in the German Imperial Navy in the Great War. Her first action was on the 30th June when she sighted the British tramp steamer Domingo de Larrinaga west of Ascension Island. The steamer was on passage from Bahia Blanca to the UK with a cargo of grain. Eight of the crew were killed in the action and thirty were transferred to the Pinguin. They landed in France on 20th November 1940 as prisoners of war.

By the time the Pinguin was sunk by HMS Cornwall on the 9th May 1941, she had sailed 59188 miles, sunk or captured 28 vessels and sunk 18068 tons by mines.

At 8.00am on the morning of 11th September 1940, the Pinguin engaged the Ben Avon from the stern and opened fire with her 6 guns. Captain Thomson immediately ordered his single gun to be manned and fire was returned.

His first shot proved to be a lucky one, being a direct hit on the ammunition hoist. It is unfortunate that this shell failed to explode, otherwise the outcome of the action would have been very different. Both ships kept up a heavy rate of fire but the Ben Avon, with only one gun, was gradually overpowered.

A direct hit on Ben Avon's gun put it over the side along with the gun crew. The Pinguin then moved in for the kill and the

Ben Avon was finished. Within half an hour she was on fire with her superstructure riddled with shell holes and all lifeboats destroyed. Twenty-four of her crew, including her captain and all deck officers except for one, were dead.

Captain Thomson had bravely fought his ship to the last in what must be the best of maritime traditions. He never left the bridge of the ship. He remained there directing the survivors to abandon ship. There is no doubt that the Ben Avon made a very gallant stand against the German surface raider. She was one of the few ships that dared to do so. The Pinguin fired a total of 59 shells at the ship and most of them hit.

The Ben Avon was sunk in the position 26°S 51°E which is 366 miles south west of Reunion Island in the Indian Ocean. From a crew of over 50 men, 7 British and 18 Chinese were made prisoners of war. They were transferred to a prison ship and landed at Bordeaux where they remained for five weeks.

They spent the remaining war years in the Merchant Navy prisoner of war camp Marlag und Milag Nord. Captain Thomson is commemorated on Panel 16 of the Tower Hill memorial in London. The Ben Line lost a total of 14 ships during the war through enemy action.

Able Seaman William Rosie

Able Seaman William B Rosie served with the Merchant Navy on the SS Radhurst.

His parents were Alexander and Arabella Rosie (née Brown). His home was at East End, St Margaret's Hope and he was born on 29th January 1907. Most of his working life was spent at sea.

The Radhurst, ex Sava, ex Nereide 24, was a general cargo vessel, built in 1910 by Cantiere Navale Triestino, Monfalcone, Italy for the Oceania Shipping Co Ltd. of Susak, Yugoslavia. She was a ship of 3403 gross tons with a speed of 9 knots and was managed by J&C Harrison of London for the Ministry of War Transport.

When navigating the St Lawrence River in Canada on the 19th July 1942, the Radhurst collided with the Norwegian cargo vessel Havørn which sank as a result.

Able Seaman William Rosie lost his life on the 20th February 1943 when his ship was torpedoed and sunk by the German submarine U525 (Kapitan Leutnant Hans Joachim Drewitz) at midnight 19th/20th February. The Radhurst sailed from the Tyne in ballast on the 13th January 1943, bound for New York, first calling at Loch Ewe and then the Clyde where she awaited the formation of Convoy ONS 165. The convoy left the Clyde on the 2nd February and was due to arrive at New York on the 28th. The ship was last reported on the 19th February when she became separated from the convoy in a gale.

A cargo ship with a speed of 9 knots sailing alone without escort was very easy prey for a waiting enemy submarine. The position given places the ship about 200 miles NNE of St John's, Newfoundland. She carried a crew of 38 seamen and 4 gunners. There were no survivors.

A total of 898 ships sailed in 24 ONS (Outward North Slow) convoys during 1943. Sixteen ships were lost in convoy and a further 3 were listed as straggler losses, one of which was the Radhurst.

The U525 was sunk on the 11th August 1943 north west of the Azores by depth charges and aerial torpedoes from an Avenger and a Wildcat aircraft from the American escort carrier USS Card. There were no survivors from the crew of 54 seamen. The U-boat is reported as having done one patrol and sinking one ship, the Radhurst.

The U525 was a type IXC/40 submarine built by Deutsche Werft AG of Hamburg and was commissioned on the 30th July 1942.

Able Seaman William B Rosie is commemorated on Panel 86 of the Tower Hill Memorial in London.

Able Seaman William Rosie.

The SS Giralda

After 5 months of war, the full reality of its horrors and brutality were vividly brought home to everyone at the end of January 1940 with a marine disaster very close to South Ronaldsay. The SS Giralda was a ship of 2178 tons belonging to Salvesens of Leith. She was a frequent visitor to Kirkwall and the crew were well known in the town.

On the morning of Tuesday 30th January 1940 she was on a voyage from Ayr to Kirkwall with a cargo of coal. About 3 miles SE of Grimness she was attacked by 2 German aircraft. She was bombed and machine-gunned and when she was well ablaze was left to her fate by her attackers. The crew launched the ship's lifeboat and abandoned ship. The incident was seen by Captain Henry Vallance, the pilot of a passing Scottish Airways aircraft. He saw the plight of the seamen and flew over them waving encouragement. When he landed in Kirkwall he reported what had happened and it wasn't long before a crowd gathered on the shore at Grimness to watch the unfolding events.

There was a heavy sea running and the watchers on shore, who included the doctor, nurse, policeman and coastguards, were horrified to see the boat capsize in the surf about 1/4 mile from the shore. The Longhope Lifeboat was called out but because of the distance involved, it was too late in arriving. The Giralda carried a crew of 23 and all were lost. The bodies could be seen coming in through the surf at Honeysgeo and, no doubt in the hope that there may yet have been life, courageous attempts were made to reach them and bring them on shore. A daring rescue bid was made by Lieutenant Barnett of the Royal Corps of Signals. He removed some of his clothing and, with a rope tied around him, he swam out through the icy cold water. Others at the scene did what they could to help, and among them were John Cromarty of South Cara and Archie Bichan of the Head. Both men had given valuable assistance and had endangered their own lives attempting to save others.

The Cromarty Hall in St Margaret's Hope was used as a temporary mortuary as it had been some months earlier for some of the bodies from HMS Royal Oak. Seven of the crew of the Giralda were from Shetland and two bodies were returned to the islands for burial. The body of the ship's master, Captain Rasmusen, and two others were sent to Leith. The remaining eighteen bodies were buried at St Olaf's Cemetery in Kirkwall on Sunday 4th February 1940 in what must have been one of the largest funerals to be held there.

In July 1940 there was a dramatic sequel to the loss of the SS Giralda. The bravery of the two local men, Archie Bichan and John Cromarty, was recognized when they were each presented with a medal.

The proceedings started with a military parade in the Cromarty Square which moved to the tennis court where the presentation of the medals took place before a large gathering of local people and servicemen. It was a fine summer's day but some banks of fog were hanging around. The ceremony had gone well and the medals had been presented by the Lord Lieutenant of Orkney, Mr. Alfred Baikie of Tankerness, when explosions were heard nearby and an enemy aircraft roared overhead and disappeared out over the bay. The Luftwaffe pilot was clearly visible as he flew low over the tennis court. The first bombs fell in Widewall and the last just below Quoyangry, in a direct line with the tennis court. It was reported that twenty bombs fell on this occasion.

The ceremony had a very rapid ending and everyone quickly scattered. There was a distinct possibility that the aircraft may have been the first of several, but, as it turned out, it was a lone intruder. If the bombs had been released two or three seconds later, the results would have been horrific. A good number of those present would not have returned to their homes alive and there would have been many a sad home in South Ronaldsay. It was certainly an incident which to this day has never been forgotten by anyone who was there.

This leaves an unanswered question. How did this lone German bomber happen to fly directly over the gathering of people, right in the middle of the proceedings? Was it just a coincidence? If it was, it was a huge coincidence. It may have been damaged in combat or it may have developed a fault and the crew may have jettisoned their bomb load in an attempt to gain height.

But equally, they may just have released the bombs that few seconds too soon. There is another possibility which can't be completely ignored. Could the hand of an enemy agent have been behind it? There were many stories of German spies at that time. It is a question which cannot be answered now. It was reported that the aircraft did not return to its base. It was shot down by fighters from RAF Wick, although this has not been confirmed.

This was an incident, early in the war, which made everyone realise that the conflict could and would be brought right to their homes. This time the war was not to be fought hundreds of miles away in the trenches and mud of France and Flanders. With Norway in German hands, Orkney was well within range of the Luftwaffe.

Presentation to Archie Bichan.

Presentation to John Cromarty.

Postscript

It is now almost eighty years since Alex Carrick's statue was dedicated to the memory of the young men of the island who proudly donned the King's uniform and marched away to the horrors of the trenches of France and Flanders. Most of them were volunteers, young men in the prime of life. They went away to live and fight in conditions which were unimaginable to their families at home. No doubt the motivation which inspired them was a strong sense of patriotism, a search for adventure and with many friends and acquaintances in uniform it is possible that peer pressure was also a factor. It was just the right thing to do at that time.

The memorial is kept in good condition. The stonework has been cleaned and the lettering re-painted whenever necessary. The ground it stands on was gifted to the community and now legally belongs to the Community Council who are responsible for maintenance.

The Kirkwall branch of the Royal British Legion have in recent years arranged a competition for the best kept war memorial in the county and South Ronaldsay has been the winner on several occasions.

There is a parade each year on Armistice Sunday attended by ex-servicemen and various youth organisations. As the years pass by it is inevitable that the number of ex-servicemen who are able to attend will become fewer.

At the end of the war Britain had a large empire to be garrisoned and protected. The men who had served during the war had to be demobilised. They had had enough of service life and were desperate to return to their families, homes and civilian occupations. The number of regular servicemen available was insufficient to meet the needs of the country and conscription continued until November 1960. Many of the young men of the island were called up and served, mainly in the Army and the Royal Air Force.

The country was involved in many incidents throughout the world during the post-war years of conscription. The British Army on the Rhine and the Berlin Airlift required a large number of men, and then the Korean War in 1950 along with terrorist activities in various parts of the Empire demonstrated the need for the Armed Forces to be fully manned and well maintained.

Bibliography

Arge N J   - Stridsarini
Banks Arthur   - A Military Atlas of the First World War
Bowyer Chaz   - Bomber Barons
Falls Cyril   - Armageddon 1918
Farrie Lt Col Angus   - Queens Own Highlanders
Forty George   - The Royal Tank Regiment
Hague Arnold   - The Allied Convoy System 1939-1945
Haldane Lt Col M M   - A History of the 4th Battalion Seaforth
                                    Highlanders

HMSO   - British Merchant Vessels Lost or Damaged
                                    by Enemy Action during the 2nd World War
Hogg Ian V   - Dictionary of World War I
Jordan Roger   - The World's Merchant Fleets 1939
Lingwood & O'Donognue   - The Trades Increase
Livesey Anthony   - The Viking Atlas of World War I
Lloyds War Losses   - The Second World War
McIntyre Colin.   - Monuments of War
Middlebrook Martin   - The Kaiser's Battle
Middlemiss N L   - Gathering of the Clans
Miller David   - U Boats History, Development & Equipment
                                    1914-1945
Perrett Bryan   - Through Mud and Blood
Rohwer J &Hummelchin G   - The Chronology of War at Sea 1939-45
Rohwer Jurgen.   - Axis Submarine Successes in World War II
Rosignoli Guido   - The Allied Forces in Italy 1943-45
Slader John   - The Fourth Service & The Red Duster at
War
Spicer-Hurd Sir Archibald   - The Clan Line in The Great War
Stewart Lt Col J. DSO   - The Fifteenth (Scottish) Division 1914-1919
                                    and John Buchan
Warner Philip   - The Battle of Loos
Woodman Richard   - Arctic Convoys

The Ben Line Book.
Family letters and records
Back numbers of The Orcadian and Orkney Herald
Battalion and Squadron War Duties
Regimental Records